Contents

CHANGING YOUR JOB

KING ALFRED'S COLLEGE
WINCHESTER

———

To be returned on or before the day marked
below :—

MAY 18 1985		
20. JUN. 1986		

Changing Your Job

Godfrey Golzen & Philip Plumbley

Kogan Page

First published 1971 by
Kogan Page Limited
120 Pentonville Road
London N1 9JN

Copyright © 1971, 1974, 1978, 1981
by Godfrey Golzen and Philip Plumbley
All rights reserved

Second impression 1972
Third impression 1973
Second (revised) edition 1974
Reprinted 1975
Third (revised) edition 1978
Fourth (revised) edition 1981

Printed in Great Britain by
The Anchor Press Ltd and bound by
Wm Brendon & Son Ltd,
both of Tiptree, Essex

ISBN 0 85038 408 7 (Hb)
ISBN 0 85038 409 5 (Pb)

Preface to the Fourth Edition

Since this book was first written over ten years ago, career change has become almost an accepted part of what some writers have described as the 'mid-life crisis'. For some people a job or even a career switch after their mid-30s is a way out of a rut or stalemate. For others it is an involuntary process, brought on by economic changes or changes in management style, philosophy or simply ownership in the companies for whom they have been working. This book is applicable equally to both groups of people, although it is primarily written for the latter because the evidence is that not enough is being made available to them in the way of organised help and advice — though the situation is certainly better than it was in 1971 when the first edition of this book appeared under the title *Changing Your Job After 35*. Perhaps this is a reflection of the fact that, as a recent Institute of Personnel Management survey showed, a great many companies still do not like to face the idea of executive redundancy. The survey, which was published under the title of *Executive Redundancy*, was based on a significantly and unusually poor response from member companies; and of those who did respond 40 per cent had no formal policies in this sphere. This did not mean that executives in those companies who had the misfortune to be made redundant were treated badly. On the contrary, they were very much better treated than lower-paid employees or than specified by the meagre provisions that redundancy legislation sets out; the feeling being that more senior people had not only made an investment in commitment to their company which deserved more than token recognition but that they would also find it more difficult than younger or less well-paid members of staff to find other employment at the same levels. This being the

7

case, it is all the more surprising that in other than financial respects redundant executives are often left to sink or swim by their employers. The survey shows that counselling and redeployment services are available but, with notable exceptions, few employers show any initiative in helping people through what may be the most difficult period some of them have ever had to face: psychologically, materially and in terms of meeting unfamiliar situations such as job interviews.

Broadly speaking, that is the objective of this book. That it has successfully met a need is shown by its sales through its several editions and the fact that it is used in a number of courses for executives on handling redeployment and is recommended in a number of IPM publications, including the latest one on *Executive Redundancy*, published in 1980, to which we have referred. We have, therefore, seen no need to make changes in the general principles of the book, but there are a great many changes of detail that have been incorporated in the new edition — changes in the facts and figures in the legislation and changes in the social and economic environment which we have wished to take into account.

One thing we would have liked to change, the need for which has been pointed out to us by a number of readers, is that the book appears to be aimed at a mainly male audience. The fact that executives are referred to as 'he' is a reflection of the fact that to include the words 'or she' in every instance would have made for clumsy reading. Furthermore, it must be said that since 1971 the number of women in executive jobs has grown enormously and this book is for them as much as for men. We believe their problems, and the way of approaching those problems, to be the same as for men. Indeed we are dismayed to note that the IPM survey shows that an attitude persists among companies that women are less hard hit by the effects of redundancy than men. In a limited way and in a material sense this may be true of married female executives, but in general it is an attitude which cannot be justified either by the facts or by the social circumstances reflected in such legislation as the Equal Pay and Sex Discrimination Acts.

Once again the authors would like to acknowledge the constructive comments, verbal and written, made by executives, consultants and professional institutes. Particular thanks are due to Mr M J Hele, who has contributed a section on selection boards; to Miss Nicola Kingston, formerly of the BIM, for supplying a number of factual items; to Mr J J Q Fox of Career Analysts for his advice on Chapter 3 ('A Personal Stocktaking'), and to the Director of Information at the DHSS for suggestions and comments on Chapter 2.

London, April 1981

Godfrey Golzen
Philip Plumbley

1. Facing up to Change

Recognising change when one is living with it is sometimes very difficult. Recently a postcard was discovered which had been sent to England by a British lady living in Moscow in October 1917, the month the Russian Revolution broke out. It said something like 'The weather is still beautiful but we seem to be having a spot of bother in the streets.' Many people who have picked up this book will recognise the similarity between their position and that of this anonymous witness of events 60 years ago, because in its way the period of technological change which we are now going through and the shift of economic power from the industrialised nations to those which are rich in resources is as drastic as the Russian Revolution. But as at that time it is only gradually that an awareness has come that things are radically not as they were — in our case that jobs which were once thought safe are no longer so; that firms which are regarded as household names can be very vulnerable, and that skills which their owners thought were good for a working lifetime have been shown to be obsolescent.

In the course of this period of transition — it has been going on now for a decade and may well last to the end of the century — some people have simply been overrun by events and have seen whole sectors of industry and the jobs that go with them disappear virtually from one year to the next. Others have anticipated change or are now in the process of doing so. Others still are in the process of changing their jobs for a variety of reasons which may or may not be connected with the times we live in. Perhaps they may feel that their firms are not keeping up with the competition and that they ought to move while they are still young enough to do so; perhaps they are aware they are not being fully stretched; perhaps the paths to promotion are slow or blocked; perhaps the money is not good enough; or perhaps they are simply bored with doing more or less the same thing in more or less the same surroundings for the foreseeable future.

You have probably picked up this book either because you are an active participant in change or because you are a victim of it. It is addressed to both groups, but you may well ask what they have in common. Simply this. Whatever your circumstances, the principles of job-finding in mid-career are basically the same, and they are very different and in some ways much more tricky than finding your earlier jobs ever was. At that time your salary would have been a great deal less than it is now, and your responsibilities in the company much less crucial. Now your commitments and expectations imply a position in which your salary is probably the least part of any loss your prospective employers might sustain if you 'don't work out'. At this point in your career, whatever your reasons for making a move, you have to prepare yourself much more intensively for the job-finding process than you did earlier on, because you are now trying to persuade some company or other to make an investment which in direct and indirect terms may run into hundreds of thousands of pounds. Furthermore, if you are now in your mid-30s or over you are likely in any case to find the job scene very much more competitive than it was when you began your first job straight out of school or university. At the time of writing Britain happens to be in the middle of a particularly severe recession, but even when this ends it is generally thought there will be fewer employment opportunities around and that there is likely to be a permanent pool of five to six per cent of the working population who will be looking for a job. Of course that does not mean that they will be the same five or six per cent, but it does mean that there will be plenty of people available and probably at all levels. Employers will be in a buyer's market for some time to come, though there will always be a demand for really good staff and for those with qualifications in fields that are 'hot' at the time. These, incidentally, may not be the same from one period of time to the next. For instance, in the early 1970s a mass of legislation created a demand for good industrial relations managers. In the mid-70s the search was for financial talent, and currently it appears that really good marketing persons are much sought after. To say that there will always be room for really good people may sound like the greatest truism of all time, but it is a fact which job-seekers sometimes seem to lose sight of. They have got so used to living with their own abilities and strengths that they tend to undervalue them, or equally to sell themselves short in an almost literal sense. A great part of this book is about how to recognise your own talents and skills and how to market them.

When should you move?

Every step in this process involves preparation, analysis and evaluation and the executive planning a move of his own accord should begin by analysing the reasons why he wants to go. Apart from the fact that he should be clear in his own mind that this is not just a question of the grass looking greener on the other side of the fence, it is likely to be one of the first questions a prospective employer will want to ask him. It would be difficult − even if it were desirable − to profile an ideal situation to move out of, but here are some questions you might ask yourself about your present situation.

1. Are your qualifications and experience being fully used where you are?
2. Is your expertise easily transferable or is it concerned with particular, specialised techniques that will narrow your area of choice?
3. If you have a particular skill or professional qualification, eg a facility in another language or an accountancy qualification, are you up to date or have your basic tools of trade become rusty?
4. Are your salary and fringe benefits generally in line with jobs of similar seniority and responsibility that you see advertised?
5. Is promotion to senior posts made mainly from within your company, or does it tend to look outside for fresh blood?
6. What job in your present company do you really want and is it likely that you would get it within an acceptable space of time?
7. Have you got everything out of your present job, or is

13

there further useful experience you might still gain there?

8. When did you last change jobs? How many changes have you made in the last ten years? Progressive moves at three- or four-year intervals can be a plus factor. But excessive restlessness, or a long time spent in one job doing the same sort of thing, will both need explaining when it comes to the interview.

9. Would you really enjoy a change of surroundings and the challenge of doing something new? Without any other advantage or motive, money alone is a poor reason for moving, unless you are grossly underpaid (ie more than 15 per cent out of line with similar jobs).

10. Is a move practicable at your age? After the mid-40s finding another job becomes increasingly difficult.

11. Would you be prepared to move to another geographical location? How would your family take it?

The last question is relevant not only to people whose jobs take them abroad — and this is happening increasingly as vacancies in the UK have become scarce and the demand, and money, appears to be abroad in the EEC, Middle East, Africa and other developing countries — but to any executives who are thinking of returning home after a spell overseas. There could be a lot of good reasons for such a move — personal and family ones, as well as the desire to get back to the hub of things in terms of one's career — but after a long spell abroad broken by well-paid periods of tax-free leave at home there could be a tendency to lose sight of the realities of everyday living in the UK. Salaries, for instance, are apt to be lower and taxation much higher than in many overseas posts; and those house prices you checked on your last trip home may have gone up considerably in the interval. Remember also that it is going to take time to find the right job unless you are exceptionally lucky and that in the meantime you are going to be living off capital. A careful assessment of such factors as these is essential, and they are dealt with more fully in Chapter 4.

The involuntary move

Sometimes, of course, change may be wholly or partially involuntary. Employers, too, have to face the fact that a man who was right for the job when he was taken on a decade ago may not possess the range of skills and qualifications needed to meet a new situation. For instance, a sales manager who was excellent at dealing with staff and customers on a person-to-person basis may be less at home with the kind of sophisticated analytical marketing skills that are called for as the company grows. Equally important is the effect on companies themselves of technological change which, for many smaller firms, may present an insoluble dilemma. To ignore it may court disaster. To participate, writing off thousands of pounds worth of plant and machinery and reinvesting in new plant that may itself have a short life cycle, is often beyond their means. In the end the choice is either one of sitting tight and becoming gradually less competitive or seeking a merger with a bigger company. Both courses of action are generally bad news for at least some executives. It would be hard to think of a merger that has not forced the new management to make a choice, in the end, between good men doing the same work. Someone always has to go.

In actual fact employers are very reluctant to take this step in the case of their more senior staff, according to the recent IPM survey on executive redundancy. The crunch does, however, tend to come in a recession and then it is not only executives whose jobs have become marginal that are let go, but whole sectors of corporate activity come under scrutiny — particularly those which do not produce an actual cash flow. Such activities are often marked by a high 'think' — and consequently executive — content: R and D, advertising, public relations and the pioneering of new products and markets.

Being out of a job is traditionally something many executives have thought of as being somebody else's problem. Redudancy, or, more brutally, the sack, rarely affected managers except the incompetent, the dishonest or the desperately unlucky. That may have been the case up to 20 years ago, but it is certainly no longer true now. The recent survey by the Institute of Personnel Management shows that only a small minority of jobless executives were dismissed for personal shortcomings. The rest are simply there because the climate for executives' careers has changed drastically since they embarked on them 10, 15 or 20 years ago. The rewards are higher than ever. However, not only have economic conditions become more unstable, but the market for executive skills has become much more volatile and competitive. Companies, like private individuals, are more apt these days to chop and change and experiment with their personnel and this is a fact of life that one simply has to adjust to.

So if change is being, or looks like being, forced upon you, the first thing you must do is rid your mind of any outdated concepts you may have about being 'out of a job'. On the one hand this means dismissing any leanings you might have towards regarding redundancy, or the prospect of it, as something to be apologetic or defensive about or as a sign to the world at large that you have failed or been at fault. On the other hand, you should realise that whatever position you have held, whatever achievements you may have to your credit and however impressive the letters after your name, in today's circumstances employers are not going to be beating a path to your door. A concerted marketing effort on your part is essential to get your foot back on the ladder. This means that you will have to make a specific inventory of your skills, to analyse who needs them and to present them, in writing and in interviews, in such a way that an employer will be persuaded that even in a period of economic uncertainty you are going to be a worthwhile investment for him. This applies whether you have chosen change or whether change has picked you out. The principal aim of this book is to give you some guidelines, based on practical experience, on how to do these things effectively.

Starting the search

There are seldom any short-cuts through the long and wearisome process of filing applications and attending interviews; having made up your mind to move — whatever the reason — it is never too soon to start your search. That an opportunity will fall into your lap is possible — you may be approached by a head-hunter — but the job you want rarely comes up when you want it. Many executives with a record of solid achievement behind them have received tentative approaches from other firms during their careers; the chief executive of a rival may have invited them out to lunch one day and said out of the blue 'If you're ever thinking of moving, I hope you'll let us know.' That kind of contact will be useful to you, as we shall show later, but it does not usually mean there is a job being permanently held open for you at X's. Most businessmen like to feel that they have 'first call' on a good person's services should they become available, but this is often big talk and too much reliance should not be placed on it. Companies control their head count much more vigorously these days.

The man who thinks his job might be in danger is particularly apt to be a victim of his own illusions, and because he may only have a limited amount of time in which to get resettled it is wise to be absolutely clear-minded about the realities of the situation. Sometimes such a man cannot bring himself to believe the facts, or if he does, he hopes they will go away. He has had 10 or 15 years' service with this company. He has a record of solid achievement in heading what he believes to be one of its important divisions. Surely they cannot afford to waste his talents? Surely, having given some of the best working years of his life to their service, they will look after him? It is not being cynical to say – don't bank on it. In such circumstances, you can reasonably hope for adequate compensation, but not that a post will be 'found' for you. Indeed, the more senior your position, the more difficult it is for the board to do this – quite apart from the fact that such jobs often disappear in the next stage of reorganisation.

Another common error is made by the man who sees trouble coming, who even has taken to scanning the papers for jobs, but who feels there is no hurry. Every week there seems to be a lot of posts for which he is well qualified and which he would presumably stand a good chance of getting. So why rush out now? The situation may get better; he may even get an offer from somebody else if he drops a few hints around the place. Besides, he hasn't seen anything that's absolutely right for him yet. The fact is, though, that when he really starts trying he is likely to find things much tougher than he had imagined. It is reckoned by executive placement consultants that a man between 35 and 45 may take between four and nine months to find a new executive job at this level; and that the over-45s may have to spend as much as two years in their search, unless they are prepared to lower their sights quite appreciably. Even those firms that give what they consider to be ample warning to an executive who is to be made redundant seldom take full account of the time it takes nowadays for a senior man to relocate himself satisfactorily.

We are talking here, of course, of the executive who would prefer to stay where he is. Assuming you are in this position, at what stage should you make up your mind that the omens are definitely running against you to the point where you must start doing something about it? Once again, it would be difficult to profile a specific situation of this kind, since the circumstances vary from case to case. There are, however, some situations that carry the seeds of a redundancy threat and among the more common ones are the following:

1. It is generally reckoned that a person in a senior job in a company that is taken over is in an exposed position because the parent firm will sooner or later want its own protégés in policy-making areas. Executives who have been vocal in their opposition to a takeover are, of course, particularly vulnerable.

2. Mergers between two companies in the same field produce overlaps between services, such as sales forces, which are an obvious target for the rationalisation of personnel.

3. The closing down of a division, a part of an operation or an overseas office will affect not only the people who have been working in it directly but those who have been providing liaison and other central services.

4. A record of declining or marginal profitability in a company or division, particularly at a time of general economic pressure, may lead to closure or at least to a thinning out of executive staff — even if they themselves are meeting the objectives they have been set within the general framework.

5. Close association with the policies of a direct superior who has been removed from office after a boardroom row, or who has simply been transferred to another part of the organisation, often begins by making the people concerned suspect to the new regime and ends by putting them in an untenable position.

These general signs will be accompanied, in the first instance, by a change of attitude towards the executive concerned by top management — or by his colleagues if he is on the board himself. Whatever management may say, if you know that return on capital employed is inadequate or that ratios are poor, standards set lax, or cash at the bank and resources underused, take care — the writing is on the wall for those able to read and interpret it. Everyone is familiar with the horror stories of the men who come to take your carpet away, or of the executive who returns after the weekend to find that someone else has moved into his office. In real life, or at least in a civilised business climate, the signs are apt to be more subtle, if no less dangerous. The possibilities of signalling such situations are obviously legion but there are a number of familiar ploys:

1. allocation to a special assignment or project which is plainly removed from the real source of action;
2. unexpected delays and barriers put in the way of obtaining sanction for necessary items of expenditure on staff and equipment;
3. the appointment of subordinates to your staff without proper consultation;
4. the appointment of an associate who, while nominally parallel to you, is in fact plainly enjoying a much fuller degree of management confidence than you are. This will manifest itself in such ways as his being called to attend policy-making meetings that you have attended regularly in the past.

Handling the transition period

Among the situations we have just described may be ones that you recognise as being your own. But if you are still working and have not been warned of redundancy, one thing you must try to avoid absolutely is any sort of confrontation over the issues with which you are dissatisfied because, if there is no time at which it is too early to begin your job search, there is equally no point at which it is wise to endanger your present job until the moment when your next one is signed, sealed and settled. You may find your present circumstances humiliating and infuriating. Do not let this show in your attitude and do not complain about it to superiors, colleagues or subordinates. Keep your problems to yourself (though you may find it a relief to blow off steam about them to an understanding spouse or close friends) but in the office act as if everything was perfectly normal. Collect your salary and do your job as efficiently and wholeheartedly as you have always done. In the meantime look for a change with all the means at your disposal. You should also bear in mind that when you do move it should be within the context of an ordered career structure, at least as far possible; that is to say, you should have assessed your strengths and weaknesses and your personal and financial goals and you should be acting within that framework. In other words, don't panic. An impulsive bad move, made for no other reason than the understandable desire to shake the dust of your present surroundings off your shoes, could upset what has, up to now, been a soundly built progression of jobs.

The fact that, for the moment, you are lying low does not make you a doormat. There will be a time to throw down the challenge about policy differences or a colleague with whom you disagree — when you have another job to go to if you lose the argument, not before.

Coping with the stress of unemployment

If you have already lost your job or if you have made up your mind to resign from what you feel is an intolerable position you will, in the normal course of events, have to face a period of unemployment. How long that is likely to be depends mostly on your age — all authorities agree that the older you are, the longer it will take, even if you have excellent qualifications. In the next chapter we will deal with the problem of coping with some of the material aspects of the situation, but the psychological aspects are equally important.

In recent years there has been quite a lot of research into how executives react to being unemployed, and you will probably recognise some of the symptoms: numbness, broken by spells of euphoria and relief at having got shot of it all; anger and resentment at your employers, the world in general and possibly yourself for not having seen the writing on the wall sooner, and finally adaptation — knuckling down to such matters as preparing your cv, making contacts, writing off for jobs, going for interviews and possibly following some of the suggestions made in this book and by your friends for filling in waiting time. These phases will not follow each other in an orderly progression — the anger and resentment syndromes will recur over such almost inevitable setbacks as being shortlisted for a job and then not getting it — but the important thing is to get back to an adjusting frame of mind as soon as possible.

One aspect of this process of adjustment relates to your financial position. While we would not advocate taking a drop in salary if it can possibly be avoided, it is worth asking yourself — should your income expectations be proving to be a barrier to re-employment — whether these expectations are totally realistic. As a successful executive you have developed tastes and demands for yourself that reflect your status and salary: a large house, a good car, holidays abroad, expensive clothes, regular entertainment and so forth. Undeniably, it is extremely hard for a person to face up to the possibility that he may have to lower his sights to the extent of doing without some of these things, not only for material reasons, but out of pride and because, in an affluent society, we tend to see them as the outward symbols of one's place on the social ladder — and even, psychologically, as the marks of masculinity and success. But there comes a point when you should ask yourself whether you are attaching an importance to them that is not only born of assumptions that are in themselves open to question, but which stand in the way of your real need at this point — getting a job that will give you a position from which to fight back. Ability will out, and it is a quality for which employers are always looking. With the maturity, judgement and all-round business know-how which you command you should feel optimistic about your chances of making your mark in any organisation you join, even if you come in at a level below what you have been used to.

Inevitably the process of adjustment will also involve your family and friends. Sad but true to relate, there have been cases of executives who, having lost their jobs, have kept up a pretence of going to work rather than tell people what has happened. That would be an extreme reaction, but there have been plenty of instances where the absence of sensible discussion within the family has produced a situation where a spell of unemployment has been taken either too lightly or, conversely, with undue despondency. Without making a drama of it, the implications should be brought into the open within the family. Points to be taken into consideration could include the following:

1. Who should be told and how?
2. How much cash or realisable assets do you have?
3. What are your essential commitments — eg food, clothes, household expenses? How long will your reserves last in relation to these?
4. What is the effect of losing such fringe benefits as a car and an expense account? Which of them must be replaced immediately?
5. What luxuries could you sacrifice without much hardship or loss of morale?
6. What nonessential commitments do you have? They may range from a booked holiday which can be cancelled to much weightier considerations such as school fees and club memberships.

The obvious question at this point is how long it is likely to be before you find another job, not only because of its financial implications but because one major problem for the formerly busy executive is that there is nothing worthwhile to do most of the day. DIY, the garden and hobbies cease to be satisfying after a while and it is hard to concentrate when watching every post. You feel that you must hurry things along, so you start phoning the consultants or employers. If this is done carefully it can be helpful but constant chivvying will do you harm. Their timescale is different from yours, not because they are dilatory but because they have to fit in with other busy people. It may be helpful if you bear in mind the following typical timescale of events: from enquiry to firm assignment — at least two weeks; from brief to appearance of an advertisement — two weeks; a search consultant's 'desk search', ie scanning of company records, reference books, gathering information about people with good or poor reputations in the industry, and identifying possible candidates — up to four weeks; receiving and sifting replies to an advertisement — two weeks; arranging/interviewing possible candidates — two to three weeks; drawing up a shortlist and writing reports — one week; time taken by employer to see shortlist — one to four weeks; decision/further interview/ negotiation/reference checking — one to six weeks. The more senior the job the more difficult it is to arrange meetings and get decisions. Typically, from decision to recruit to offer takes in total from (very exceptionally) four weeks to six months.

So what do you do when time is heavy on your hands? If you can come to terms with the timescale above you will see that you are likely to have x weeks, as opposed to an endless succession of days, in which to plan to do something useful. This may take the form of a course of reading, of attending courses or conferences, attending exhibitions on generally bringing yourself up to date with technology or techniques. A part-time teaching or lecturing post or agreement to write some technical articles is a great spur to further study and brings in some cash. Another useful short-time activity is a consultancy assignment or a spell of work for a charity. Keep busy if at all possible, as it provides a stimulus to the mind and keeps your cutting edge sharp — which is readily apparent at an interview (as is the converse). Don't be afraid to go on holiday if you know nothing is likely to happen for several weeks — but ensure you can be contacted easily if necessary. While minor DIY jobs soon run out or become irritating, a more major task can be absorbing and stimulating. Likewise a hobby can be developed. The dinghy sailor can become an RYA-qualified instructor, the artist start to paint seriously, the amateur musician 'stiffen' other groups for major concerts (for a fee) and so on. All of these can be relatively easily picked up or put down but if you have a goal to improve your performance in your own and in other people's eyes this can be mentally very rewarding. Another alternative for some people is casual work — drive a cab, act as a guide, drive a lorry, serve in a shop, help out in a bar or restaurant. But while these help the exchequer they can prove a tie and make attending interviews difficult, and they don't do a lot for your self-respect.

Doctors will tell you that it is very important to keep fit in times of stress. Eat less but eat wholesome food. Take plenty of exercise and keep yourself in good physical shape. This not only makes you look good but, more importantly, makes you feel alert and proud of your appearance which again will always impress an interviewer and a future employer. If you had to choose between someone who appears to have gone to seed — overweight, uncombed, dull-eyed, slow to answer, slovenly — and someone who is alert, clear-eyed and trim, with carefully cleaned and pressed clothes, which would you choose?

Stress cannot be ignored but its symptoms can be recognised for what they are. Stress builds up slowly and takes time to disappear. It is often more readily apparent to those close to you than to yourself. This is why close friends and your spouse are so important and their advice should be listened to. Obviously if things become extreme you may need medical help but the kind of stress we are talking about there can only be alleviated by drugs. The cure lies in your own hands and in the understanding of those around you. Share and talk out your troubles and then do something positive; action and business are the best aids and facing issues squarely and not letting yourself feed on them the best prevention.

2. How to Leave Gracefully - and Advantageously

There is a right and a wrong way of doing almost everything and leaving a job is no exception. Do so gracefully, because the very first step in your job hunt is to leave with the good will of your last firm.

If your search is beginning while you are still with them, it will help your morale and gain the respect of your associates if you carry on normally as far as possible — even when you are only working out a period of notice. Keep the hours you have always kept, and, if you are losing interest under the circumstances in which you find yourself, do not make this plain in your attitude to the job, your associates or the people working under you.

There will be occasions when you will want to attend interviews during office hours. When this is the case, notify anyone who may want to try and reach you while you are out. As an executive you will not have to account for your time, but, enjoying the status you do, it should be a matter of pride to make up in the office for any time you have spent in pursuing your own career. In certain cases, in fact, it may be an advantage to conduct your job search out of office hours. Formal interviews are conducted during the day, but if you are trying to arrange an informal meeting with a senior man who may have a job or a job lead for you, he is likely to have more time for you at the end of the day when the phone has stopped ringing. The fact that you are still choosing to devote all or most of your normal working hours to your present job may also be a fact that impresses him favourably. After all, that is the kind of performance he will expect from you if you join his organisation or that of somebody to whom he might recommend you.

When the time finally does come for you to leave,

circumstances will sometimes have developed so that the temptation may be to go out in a cloud of steam, having told those of your superiors and colleagues responsible for your departure exactly what you think of them. However satisfying this prospect may appear, dismiss it firmly from your mind. For one thing your future employers will almost certainly check you out with your previous company before offering you a job. If you have left a bunch of angry men behind you, their recommendations are going to be less than enthusiastic. If, on the other hand, they see departing a confident, collected individual they will probably feel they made a mistake in letting you go. Ultimately this is far more satisfying to your ego than a slanging match, but what is more important is that the last impression they have of you (and that is the one they will convey to your next employer) is of a good man going.

To reinforce this point take some time during your last couple of days to drop in on all the senior executives of the company with whom you have had more than passing contact and say goodbye to them. Keep your comments cordial and positive, along the lines that you've enjoyed working with them and that you wish them success for the future (even though such statements may be slightly short of the truth!). Don't ask for recommendations or favours, and above all do not discuss the circumstances of your leaving. If you privately feel that there may have been faults on both sides, do not apologise for any mistakes you think you might have made. It is important that you yourself should recognise them, where this is the case, but keep such matters to yourself. What's past is past and should be referred to again only in helping you to build your future.

While your superiors and colleagues are important, do not forget those who have been working under you. Their loyalty deserves this token of your recognition, but, apart from that, the strong approval of a man's subordinates tends to register favourably with his superiors and equals. This does not mean that you should try to range your staff against the company or your successor — this will not do you any good and may do them a lot of harm; their liking and respect for you will be even greater if you do not involve them in your problems.

Leaving your job on good terms does not, of course, mean that you should leave without claiming all that you are entitled to by legislation and by any contract you might have with your company. Just as, in the course of your service, you will have attempted to gain the best possible terms for your firm, you should now make sure that you yourself get a fair deal from them.

In the first place your employer has a number of basic legal obligations towards you and you should begin by checking that he has fulfilled them.

Under the Employment Protection (Consolidation) Act of 1978 the company should have given you written particulars of the terms of your engagement when you joined their service. The points in this statement that are of particular relevance to you now concern the minimum period of notice to which you are entitled, holidays, the provisions of the company pension scheme and any clauses that may set out compensation in case of severance.

Notice

In the vast majority of cases of executive redundancy, ample notice will be given, but it is worth pointing out that under the Employment Protection Act, certain minimum periods of notice are laid down which amount broadly to one week's salary for each year of continuous employment.

You may be offered the alternative of either working out your notice or taking payment in lieu. The latter prospect is, on the face of things, tempting: firstly, you may consider that it will leave you absolutely free to look for another job; secondly, remaining with the company while under notice can be a somewhat humiliating and strained situation; and thirdly, because while you are working you are being taxed at your normal rate, whereas payments relating to loss of job (including *ex gratia* payments and redundancy payments) are tax free up to a total limit of £25,000. Against this you have to consider that it is generally thought to be easier for a man to find a new job while he is still employed and this has been borne out in an Institute of Personnel Management survey. You also have to weigh up the tax advantages of taking payment in lieu against the fact that you may not be entitled to unemployment benefit until the period of notice which the payment covers has expired. In other words, if you are given four months' pay in lieu at the end of December you may not get unemployment benefit until the beginning of May.

Holidays

You should receive your salary for any holidays specified in your Contract of Employment which you have not yet been able to take. How holidays accrue, and are paid for, varies between employers, but a fair basis, if nothing is laid down, would be one that is prorated on the proportion of the year you have worked up to the point you were given notice.

Redundancy

In addition to holidays and proper notice, you may be entitled to redundancy pay —provided you have been continuously employed by your present employer for at least 104 weeks. The fact that you have been given payment in lieu of notice does not affect the entitlement. You should, however, bear in mind that you will only be eligible if you really have been declared redundant. The word is nowadays somewhat loosely used to cover the general state of being unemployed but in terms of the Redundancy Payments Provisions of the Employment Protection Act, such payment is only due if you lose your job 'through cessation or diminution of work of a particular kind in a particular place where he (ie the redundant employee) is employed'. You are not, therefore, entitled to redundancy pay if you are sacked or leave of your own accord. However, employers are encouraged to interpret redundancy as liberally as possible by virtue of the fact that the reason why the employer requires fewer employees does not affect the individual's right to be considered as redundant. This can be taken to mean that if you are running an operation that has to be closed down or curtailed because it is not producing results, your loss of office in such circumstances would count as redundancy.

If, having been given notice, you leave before that notice expires, you do not forfeit your right to redundancy payment provided you notify your employer in writing of your decision and he does not object (also in writing) to your leaving.

Unfair dismissal

If you have lost your job in circumstances where you feel you have had a raw deal from your employer, you may be able to bring a case against him for unfair dismissal, provided you have worked for him for at least 52 weeks. (If you were engaged after 1 October 1980 by a small employer — one who has employed 20 or fewer people during the whole time you were working there — you would have to have worked for 104 weeks before being able to bring a case.)

The relevant legislation is contained, once again, in the Employment Protection (Consolidation) Act of 1978 and the Employment Act of 1980. The criteria of what constitutes unfair dismissal are reasonably clear, though there are some potentially contentious areas — for instance what is and what is not a genuine redundancy — and if you think you might have a case, you can make an application on a form obtainable from your local Jobcentre. This goes to a conciliation officer who, if you wish, will either try to get your employer to reinstate you or to compensate you fully. If he cannot get agreement on compensation or you do not wish him to pursue reinstatement your case will go to an industrial tribunal. The tribunal will be guided not only by the reasons for and the circumstances of your dismissal but also by whether the employer, whatever the circumstances, has acted reasonably. An important criterion here is whether he has given you due warning over a period of time that your work has been unsatisfactory, why he considers it to be so and what you should have been doing to improve it.

If the tribunal decides in your favour and you do not want reinstatement or the employer refuses to reinstate you, the financial rewards can be considerable; the maximum compensation is £9850 and in special cases certain additional awards can bring this up to £16,000. Awards are dependent on age, salary, length of service and loss resulting from dismissal. However, it is fair to say that payments of the latter magnitude are seldom made.

Scale of redundancy pay

Compensation is based on gross earnings in the last week of employment up to a limit of £130 pw. This weekly earnings figure is multiplied by the number of years of continuous employment, up to a maximum of 20 years, with a weighting according to age. The scale likely to apply to most readers of this book is as follows:

1. between the ages of 22 and 40, for each year of continuous employment with the present employer — one week's salary;
2. between the ages of 41 and 64 (59 for women), for each year of continuous employment with your present employer — one-and-a-half week's salary.

By the standards of executive or even skilled worker salaries these amounts are not particularly generous — £1300 for a man in his late 30s with ten years' service is very little to write home about — so it has become common practice for employers to top up redundancy payments with further *ex gratia* contributions. This has become true even in the public sector, a case in point being the very large sums paid out by the British Steel Corporation to redundant employees. But the employer's statutory obligation is confined to the figures set out above. Indeed, if he wants to play it strictly by the book, he can offset any contributions he has made to your pension scheme against redundancy payments.

Fixed contracts

Many senior executives have negotiated contracts with their employers under which they receive benefits and terms of employment running well beyond the statutory ones. Inasmuch as these concern benefits in kind — use of a company car, for instance — it is usually clear that these are the property of the company, returnable once employment ceases, though many companies allow executives to keep a company car for the full term of contract/notice, and then buy it at book value. A much trickier situation can arise over clauses guaranteeing your employment at a certain salary over a fixed number of years. In most cases such agreements will be honoured, but if you are running into problems over this the best step is to consult your solicitor and show him the contract, since legal documents are sometimes open to misinterpretation by the non-expert. What is clear, however, is that even if you are due to receive compensation under a fixed-term contract you are, in most circumstances, able to claim redundancy payment as well. This will always be the case if your contract was for a period of two years or less; providing, of course, that you have been in continuous employment with that company for at least 104 weeks. If it was for longer than this, you will be eligible if the contract was entered into after 6 December 1965, and provided you did not agree in writing to forego your right to redundancy pay.

Pensions

The status of your pension, if you change your job, depends in the first instance on whether your employers — your present one and your next one — have contracted in or out of the state pension scheme which came into force in 1978. The pension under the state scheme is related to earnings and length of service. The contributions are paid by the employer and the employee through National Insurance contributions and the benefits mature after 20 years of contributions. A great many employers in the private sector have, however, chosen to opt out of the state scheme — that is, they have agreed to provide an occupational pension scheme the benefits of which must, by law, be as good as or better than those the state provides. In these circumstances, both the employer and the employee pay a lower rate of national insurance contributions but they will be paying an amount at least equivalent to the higher NI rate to a private scheme. How much the employer does pay as his share varies, but generally employees are called on to contribute something like five per cent of taxable income and the employer puts up the rest to provide benefits which obviously vary with the size of the contribution. There is also a third option, whereby the employer contracts in but has an occupational pension scheme as well, to top up the state benefits payable on retirement.

As far as the state scheme is concerned, the employee receives a personal pension from his employer of one-eightieth of his pay for each year of service. Benefits in private schemes vary, as we have said above, but an averagely generous type would provide annually two-thirds of the pay the employee was receiving at the time of retirement, plus such additional benefits as a lump sum payable to dependants in case the employee dies before retirement.

What happens if you leave your job with an employer who,

like most in the private sector, has a contracted-out occupational pension scheme — totally, or as a top-up arrangement? Broadly, you have the following options.

1. You can get back some of the contributions you have previously made, subject to a number of restrictions. Unless you are under 26 years old or have less than five years' pensionable service, you will only be able to get back contributions made before April 1975; and even then you will have to leave some of them behind to help pay for the minimum pension scheme to which you are entitled by law. You will also have to pay tax at ten per cent on any cash you get back because, of course, you received tax relief on your contributions at the time they were made.

   Whether or not it pays you to take the cash option is a matter on which you should take professional advice from a pensions consultant. For instance, if you have had a longer period of service with the firm you are leaving, the employer's contribution — which, of course, reverts to the employer, not to you when you leave before retirement — could amount to a sizeable benefit which you would be ill-advised to abandon, unless there were strong reasons for doing so. Such reasons might, however, be valid if you needed the cash value of your contributions either to fund a self-employed pension scheme or to chip into the pension scheme of your next employer if the transfer of your present scheme is too difficult.

2. You can take a deferred pension in which case you simply freeze your and your employer's contribution at the point where you leave. In due course, when you retire or die, you or your dependants will receive benefits based on the value of the contributions made up to the time they ceased to be made.

3. You can try to transfer your pension. This is probably the best option, but the problem is that your next employer's scheme may not exactly match the benefits and contributions of your present one. In fact a mismatch between two schemes can be a bar to re-employment where the prospective new employer's scheme offers very much better benefits than your present one. He may fear being put in the position of having to

pay a backlog of contributions to make up the difference to bring you in line with company policy. On the other hand, where a new employer's scheme is less good than the one you are presently under, you can make up the difference to bring you up to the required level of benefits on retirement by making additional voluntary contributions to the new scheme. These would qualify for tax relief.

4. You can take an early pension. This option is frequently offered to employees who have been made redundant close to retirement age, or as an inducement to accept voluntary redundancy. Generally it implies a lower pension because your contributions have been less than if you had worked your full term. However, in cases where employers are prepared to concede payment of the full pension, irrespective of the fact that contributions have not been made in full, it is obviously an attractive possibility.

Pensions involve a lot of money. A pension of, say, £80 a week in current terms can be worth tens of thousands of pounds seen as the interest on a lump sum. At the same time they are an exceedingly complex subject, of which the summary above is merely a broad outline. It must be stressed, therefore, that you should get professional advice on pension matters — preferably from an independent broker or consultant rather than from someone attached to an insurance company, who might possibly have an axe to grind.

Ex gratia and severance payments

Increasingly, companies are recognising the special problems of the executive made redundant in mid or late career by paying him a larger lump sum which will give him some capital to tide him over until he finds another job. This is based on such factors as age, seniority and length of service. It is not, of course, a statutory obligation to pay more than the amounts specified under the Redundancy Payments Provisions of the Employment Protection Act, so practice regarding the sums involved and how they are based varies widely between individual cases and companies. It should be noted, though, that if you are being offered more than the total you are due as payment in lieu, plus redundancy entitlement as laid down in the Act, you will not be able to claim under the Redundancy Provisions Act as well.

Where a lump sum is offered to include payment in lieu you will have to watch that it does not prejudice your entitlement to receive unemployment benefit at the earliest possible date, because, as we have seen earlier, you may not be entitled to claim such benefit until your period of notice has expired — even where, as is the case with most executives, it is longer than the minimum period laid down in the Act. Probably the best way of handling this is to agree with the employer that he should pay you the minimum notice as a separate arrangement while you are still with the company and that the *ex gratia* or severance payment should be a separate item payable after you have left their employ.

Tax position — redundancy pay and golden handshakes

Compensation for loss of office, whether it is redundancy pay, a golden handshake or payment in lieu of notice, is tax free up to a total of £25,000, and payment for loss of office overseas is absolutely free of tax, provided it relates to a full-time overseas job.

The term 'compensation' also covers gifts in kind, so if your employer is proposing to let you keep your office car, as is not uncommon, it is better to arrange to make a nominal payment for it if its value, in addition to other benefits, is likely to take you over the £25,000 limit (provided, of course, that the payment is not so nominal as to arouse suspicion of tax evasion). However, there are circumstances where long service or early termination of a service contract are involved, under which it is possible to obtain further tax relief if your golden handshake does exceed £25,000. A rather complex accountancy device known as 'top slicing' allows your terminal payment to be treated, for tax purposes, as though it was spread over a number of years and taxed separately in each of those years. It is advisable to get an accountant's advice in this situation since individual cases vary too much to give detailed guidance here.

With this proviso, it should be stressed that the figure of £25,000 is the total that is allowable. Even if split up into several payments over several tax years if it is 'in respect of the same office or employment, or in respect of different offices held under the same employer or under associated employers, this sub-section shall apply as if those payments were a single payment' and what is more the Inspector can choose which year to charge it under, which is unlikely to be to your advantage! So if you hold a number of directorships in a group of companies you cannot get away with £25,000 for each, even if it is given to you one year at a time. And if you are given the statutory redundancy payment in one cheque and a golden handshake in another it will still be treated as one sum. Or if you have your pension commuted (to give yourself some capital) this, too, will only be exempt from tax on the first £25,000 and lumped together with any other *ex gratia* payment you may receive. Note, too, that if you are in a group you cannot avoid the £25,000 limit by being made redundant by each individual company in turn! So far as we can ascertain, the only way to get more than £25,000 tax free is to be made redundant by two quite un-related employers within a tax year — in which case the Inspectorate may feel that you deserve it!

Unemployment and earnings-related benefits

You should be aware, for the purposes of the careful budgeting that will be necessary while you are out of work, of what you are entitled to claim in the way of benefits.

There is a feeling among some executives that it is demean-ing to accept aid from the State, and certainly the conditions in which this is usually administered and the whole circum-stances of rubbing shoulders with fellow claimants who are often, to say the least, a pretty mixed lot, can be a blow to one's pride. On the other hand there is really no rational basis for such an attitude. No one feels embarrassed about accept-ing the benefits of the National Health Service (often under similar circumstances!). One pays national insurance, as one pays health insurance, for precisely the same reason — that one may one day find oneself in the position of having to claim benefit from it. It is no more rational not to collect it than it would be to fail to claim from an insurance company after a motor car accident.

There is also another factor to bear in mind. If you are unemployed but do not prove the point by attending an unemployment benefit office of the Department of Employment to show that you are available for work, contributions cannot be credited to your national insurance account. This would mean that you may need to pay Class 3 national insurance voluntary contributions — £2.40 a week at present — to maintain your entitlement to pension and benefit provisions. The pros and cons of opting for voluntary Class 3 contributions are spelled out in leaflet NI 42 (National Insurance Voluntary Contributions) available from the Department of Employment.

The amounts you are entitled to are not large, but they are useful; and if, having left it, you decide you need the money after all, it will be almost impossible to make a retroactive claim. Therefore you would be well advised to go to an unemployment benefit office as soon as you become unemployed, bringing your national insurance card and your last Certificate of Pay and Tax Deducted (Form P60). You will then be informed of when you are able to claim payment and how much you are entitled to. The date when payment (and crediting of contributions) commences will not be affected by redundancy pay, but it may be affected by any payment you have received in lieu of notice or in compensation for cancellation of a fixed-term contract.

The terms, conditions and amounts of benefit are spelled out in detail in leaflets NI 12, NI 155A and NI 196 issued by the Department of Health and Social Security. But, in essence, the weekly rates of benefit there set out are as follows, as at April 1981:

Flat rate	— men under 65, single women, widows and married women under 60	£22.50
Dependants	— for one dependent adult	£13.90
	for each dependent child	£ 5.25

In the case of an unmarried man an adult dependant may be a close dependent relative other than his wife. Children, in order to qualify as dependants, have to be either

(a) under the minimum school-leaving age, or
(b) receiving full-time education at school, college or university and under the age of 19, or
(c) other children under 19 undergoing full-time training for any trade, business or profession and who are

earning no more than £2 a week after deduction of expenses.

Dependant's benefit is not payable if a wife or other adult dependant earns more than £12.75 a week (£15.60 if claimant is a man over 65 or a woman over 60).

In addition to unemployment benefit you are entitled to collect earnings-related benefit. This is scaled according to average weekly earnings in the 1979-80 tax year in the £19.50–£135 range (the latter figure being the maximum level to which the benefit is related); and in support of your claim you will need to produce your last Certificate of Pay and Tax Deducted. The scale of amounts paid is one-third of the amount by which average earnings exceed £19.50, up to a limit of £30, and ten per cent of earnings between £30 and £135. For an executive, who can be reckoned to have been earning well over this, the benefit would, therefore, not exceed £14. The supplement begins to be paid on the 13th day of unemployment and continues for up to 156 days, not counting Sundays. It should be noted that the Government plans to abolish earnings-related benefit from January 1982.

It is easy to see from these figures that an unemployed executive with two children is eligible to collect a weekly benefit of £49.90, not a lot of money, but a very helpful subsidy towards the household expenses. Nor need you feel that as a condition of receiving unemployment benefit you will be obliged to take any job the Jobcentre offers you. It is specifically stated by the DHSS that an offer of employment regarded by them as 'suitable' is 'employment in your usual, or a similar, occupation'.

Supplementary allowance

The principle that all good things must come to an end also applies to unemployment benefit and earnings-related benefit. They expire after 312 and 156 days respectively (excluding Sundays), and, as we have already pointed out, earnings-related benefit is in any case being abolished from January 1982. You can, however, requalify for unemployment benefit. To do this, you have to have worked for an employer for a period of 13 weeks and to have worked in each of these weeks for 16 hours or more. These weeks need not be consecutive, so this requirement doesn't seem very hard to fulfil.

While it is hoped that most readers of this book will never need it, there is a further source of financial aid to which you can turn — Supplementary Allowance. The circumstances under which it is paid are set out in the *Supplementary Allowance Handbook* published by HMSO. You would be well advised to study this book if you are thinking of putting in for supplementary allowance, because to some extent claims are judged on the discretion of individual DHSS officials, though there are regulations to guide them. For instance, supplementary benefit is paid to persons whose resources are judged to have fallen below their requirements, and these are quantified: £37.50 a week subsistence for a man and wife, with additional sums for children — £10.90 for each child between 11 and 15 and £7.30 per child under 11. Claims are normally taken at an interview at the local social security office, but you should note that the possession of realisable capital of over £2000 excludes a person from benefit. An owner-occupied house is not regarded as capital in this sense, but there are obviously very few people of any substance who would in fact qualify for supplementary benefit.

However, if you do get down to your last £2000 — and it does happen — and you are unhappy with the benefit awarded after making a claim, you can ask your local social security office how their answer was arrived at. If you are not satisfied with their explanation and think some mistake has been made, you can appeal against their decision. An agency such as the Citizens' Advice Bureau would be helpful in assisting you to prepare your case.

Grants for children in higher education

Though few readers of this book are likely to be able to claim supplementary allowances, there is one benefit that may be relevant to those that have a son or daughter taking a degree qualification. In that case you would be paying a parental contribution based on your salary up to the previous 5 April. If now your annual income is likely to drop by 20 per cent or more you can apply to have the grant reassessed on a 'current year' basis. This should mean that the local authority will be prepared to increase its contribution. As a first step you should contact your Chief Education Officer and inform him of the change in your circumstances.

3. A Personal Stocktaking

Looking for a job is essentially a marketing operation. As such, it begins by making an assessment of the product: what it can and cannot do, to whom it appeals, what features should be emphasised to potential buyers, where the best outlets for it are, how much the customer is willing to pay for it and what price the producer must charge in order to keep going. Perhaps you have never thought of yourself in this light, but as an executive you do, after all, represent an investment for the company that is going to employ you — a sizeable investment that can be very profitable if it works and disastrously expensive if it does not. To put the situation in its crudest terms, what it involves is being able to sell yourself; and any salesman will tell you that the man who can walk into a client's office with a thorough knowledge of his product and a clear idea how it is going to benefit the buyer stands a far better chance of success than the man who has not taken the trouble to equip himself with this knowledge.

Of course, an executive is not some inanimate product and there is another factor in this process of self-assessment that you now have to undertake. Once people have settled down in a career, around the age of 35, they tend to rub along without thinking too closely about whether or not they are making the best use of their abilities in the job they have chosen. It may be that somewhere along the line you took, or drifted into, the wrong decision.

Whatever your situation, whether you are redundant or can see the writing on the wall — or simply feel that it is time to make a move in the interests of your career — you should first take stock of your qualifications, talents and personal attributes and see whether you have been applying them in the area that is right for you — or whether the fact that you have not been doing this is in itself a contributory cause of your situation. In other words, you have to challenge every premise on which your career thinking has been based, and start from there. This involves sizing up your strengths and weaknesses, your physical and psychological needs, to what extent your personal circumstances dictate or suggest the kind of job you should go for, where you want to live and where you could bear to live, if necessary. It involves a survey of your experience and qualifications and a clear-sighted — even ruthless — assessment of yourself as a person. All this is a necessary preliminary in deciding what sort of job you should go for.

What is the best way to do this? We suggest you look at yourself dispassionately and analytically by asking yourself the following questions:

(a) What have I to offer?
(b) What sort of things do I actually enjoy doing — and how important to me is my leisure?
(c) What are my commitments in terms of finance and location?

Then, on the basis of these factors, identify a course of action.

What have you to offer?

To make an honest assessment of yourself is notoriously difficult. The best way is to come up with something that is meaningful and constructive — as opposed to the haphazard collection of illusions, and maybe self-accusations, that are probably in your mind at this moment. Start with the facts. Take a sheet of paper and write down your answers to the following.

Qualifications and training
First, consider all the formal courses of training you have ever received — what you did well in and what you found difficult to grasp. Start with school, college or university days and then go on to any courses you have attended since — professional and technical training, skills courses, management development courses and training, special projects, Open University, correspondence courses, leisure courses —

all of these will give you trends and pointers as to the nature and depth of your intellectual ability and the range and depth of the knowledge and skills you have used this ability to develop. Don't fool yourself but equally don't underestimate your abilities. Bear in mind that of itself, a good class of degree or high course pass mark means very little to an employer. It is your ability usefully to apply the knowledge and training you have received to present and future jobs that matters. Equally, if you have missed out on university or training courses but successfully held down an intellectually demanding job for several years, don't underestimate your capabilities; on the other hand don't think you know it all and are just as good as any graduate — you may still lack a flexible mind, your knowledge may be very narrow or you may be good at doing but not so hot on analysis.

From these facts you are going to be able to draw certain conclusions that have a bearing on your job search. It is obviously unlikely that you are going to want to branch out in a completely new direction, but now is your chance to make what astronauts call a 'corrective burn' to put yourself back on course. For instance, if you have a qualification in languages that you have never had a chance to use, a job which involves travelling abroad in a field of business in which you already have some experience may make you exactly the man a lot of employers are looking for. Equally, if your previous job involved accounting, quantifying or, on the other hand, communicating skills which you found it difficult to cope with, you should now be thinking about a post better suited to the natural leanings and abilities which your educational qualifications suggest. If you are thinking about a complete switch which involves taking time out to attend courses for retraining, consider how much receptivity you display towards learning something new. A clue to this will be found in your performance on courses you have attended recently and how successfully you tackle new and unfamiliar types of work.

The subject of 'courses' takes one into a field that is increasingly important for the training of the executive of today. How up to date are you, you should ask yourself, with your profession or managerial skill? The hard fact is that a lot of people, once they think they have established themselves, cease to bother to learn — or maybe they simply do not have the time. If you fall into this category, you should note the fact as a deficiency and look at possibilities to put it right. If you have been keeping yourself up to date, jot down the areas in which your special knowledge lies.

Service record

Nowadays a service record would only be relevant if you have served in the regular armed forces. In that case a good service record is an asset. The technical and administrative training you received and the contacts you made, your ability to live in a community, to survive hardship, to submit to discipline, all of these are of value in any employment. But tight discipline curbs initiative and risk taking, even in the service-management style of today, differs markedly from that in industry and commerce; and a commission does not of itself make you a good leader or manager. On the other hand, those who have been through staff college, who have been in diplomatic posts or who have an understanding of ways of life in Third World countries have much to offer, although the over-45s may find the change in environment and management style and loss of status somewhat traumatic and this should not be underestimated. Service resettlement courses make a useful contribution to the reorientation required but it is your personality make-up and adaptability that really count. If you are in the 45+ age group and your experience of service life was gained as a national serviceman, then not too much should be made of it; it's too long ago to be relevant now.

Your working life

Now we come to the heart of the exercise — your adult working life. Make a list of the jobs you have held. How long were you in each one? What was your starting and finishing salary? Why did you move? When you were promoted, did promotion come more rapidly in some kinds of positions than others? Did you ever move sideways to gain more experience, or even leave a well-paid job with limited prospects for one that was less well paid but seemed to offer a greater challenge?

What is the range and depth of your practical work experience and how transferable is it? Are there any major gaps? (It is easy to fall into one of two extremes here: either to think you are expert in everything because you have a smattering of most aspects of your function or to under-value your experience as common sense.)

Be specific about what your various jobs and positions entailed. Apart from focusing your mind on the sort of things for which you have an aptitude, it will also help you to answer questions from potential employers in later stages of the job search. Don't simply write down that you were in charge of a department of 50 people, but describe the exact nature of your responsibilities, who you reported to, how the success of the job was measured and what your achievements were during the time you filled it. Did you, for instance, increase turnover while keeping overheads down? Did you introduce new systems of financial control or streamline and simplify an existing system? Did you carry significant respon-sibilities in helping to implement your company's changes of policy or procedure — putting through a new wage payment system, or helping to supervise a changeover from manual to computerised methods? Did you gain experience of specific new products and processes? Did you represent your com-pany in any significant negotiations with outside bodies? Did you speak publicly on their behalf?

In his book *The Effective Executive*, Peter Drucker says that in consultancy assignments he tends to evaluate the quality of a firm's executives by their ability to answer such questions as these. They differentiate the man who knows and thinks about what he is doing from the one who is only going through the motions. It is a fair bet that your future interviewer will be making the same kind of judgement when he questions you about your previous record and that he will be impressed if you can give him precise, well-thought-out answers.

But of course at this stage you are not yet aiming at a specific job, but rather building up a profile of the kind of job your would be likely to do well. An essential part of this process is to look at weaknesses as well as strengths. There is no need to be ashamed of admitting the former to yourself. We all have them, but the important thing is to find a job that will give the maximum opportunity to one's strong suits and make as little call as possible on weaker areas.

Here again your performance in various kinds of jobs will

provide most of the clues, and you should do some hard thinking about the reasons for your successes and failures. Did you, for instance, do a superb job selling your company's products and services but perform rather less well when you were promoted to a managerial function? If this was so, it might indicate that administrative staff work is not really your line, or maybe that you are essentially a 'lone wolf' operator who finds it irksome to be organising other people. On the other hand, you may have made an unsuccessful move from an office job to sales and found that the give-and-take of direct contact with customers and clients does not come so easily to you; or your last job may have meant involvement with a kind of product with which you were not at ease. Although all kinds of business activities are more or less the same in their basic principles, in some areas, such as sales, a man who spent half his working life in consumer goods is liable to find the switch to, say, capital equipment quite bewildering. So what you should try and do is to use the wisdom of hindsight to identify the kind of job at which you were successful and happy.

What sort of person are you?

How well you performed as an executive and in what capacity you are most effective is not only related to your intellectual grasp or the depth of your qualifications. It is also a matter of what sort of person you are, as this is an important aspect of the process of self-assessment. It is also a tricky one in which you can easily end up with a useless list of highly subjective evaluations. The best way to approach it is to consider yourself in action. What types and levels of people can you mix with freely and intimately, or occasionally? Visualise yourself in a typical business/management/board meeting; dealing with customers, staff or workpeople; at home, at the club. Try to distinguish the type of role you tend to take or gravitate to and the attributes other people ascribe to you. For example, in formal situations such as at work you may be valued mostly for your technical expertise; but this may be because you have never yet had the opportunity to show that you have the requisite skills for general management; on the other hand you may be a very successful chairman of the parish council in your home village where people look to you for the lead in informal situations. What is your own style of management? Are you people- or production-oriented? Do you lead, drive or arbitrate? Who decides? Try to recall what other people have said or written about your dealings with staff. Can you influence your fellow directors? If so, in what type of situation or issue? Can you influence other line managers over whom you have no authority? How are you regarded in the boardroom? As a technical expert? As a person with a good analytic brain? As a shrewd negotiator in face-to-face situations? As the executive the unions will listen to? As a maverick?

In the social or sports club do you tend to be secretary, chairman, treasurer or member? Even your family life has some bearing on the question. Are you authoritarian, or tolerant and easy-going? Psychologists view people in behavioural terms — the way in which an individual tends to behave in certain types of situations can be predicted from his behaviour in another set of analogous circumstances. That should be the aim of this stage of your self-assessment. Thus if you are basically a shy, sensitive person — no matter how well you have learned to compensate for it — avoid selling; you are unlikely to succeed there. If you can't take tough decisions about people without lying awake at night you should think twice about going into a job which involves a strong element of hiring and firing. If you work best at a job which involves a lot of variety, you will not be happy doing something which means intense concentration on one task over a long period. Are you, in general terms, intellectual, practical, physically active, decisive or cautious? Are you outgoing, or a bit of a loner? Are you creative or analytical? All these attributes (and you will be able to think of many others in connection with yourself) can be an asset; they can also be a disadvantage. It is up to you to identify the situation in which the former will hold true.

Interaction with other people

The question of relationships with colleagues is one you should look at carefully. Every commercial undertaking or worthwhile business organisation is ultimately dedicated to making a profit but most of them have their own style in the way they set about it and attract people who fit that style. Some, for instance, pride themselves on their informality, so that a person with a somewhat conventional outlook on things may come to feel out of place. The reverse is also true. A man who regards the niceties of dress and conventional behaviour as being of secondary importance to doing a good job is unlikely to be taken on by an organisation which favours white shirts and short-back-and-sides haircuts. So you should now consider your appearance, speech and manner. Show as 'strengths' the types and levels of people to whom you are readily acceptable; as 'limitations' those who from experience tend to reject you; you should also note any factors relevant in social situations such as a stammer or a rough accent. The fact that some attribute or other makes it unlikely that you will get on well with certain individuals or groups of people is not necessarily a disadvantage, but to a potential employer or interviewer it will be important, one way or the other. Your accent, for instance, would not matter in the slightest if you were applying for a job as a works manager, but it might affect your eligibility for a post involving high-level negotiations.

But while, in the much freer society we live in nowadays, externals are on the whole less important than they used to be, the basic currency of human relationships remains the same. In other words, there are still fools who occasionally have to be borne gladly, touchy superiors (not to mention superiors' wives) to be humoured and a lot of individual foibles to be handled with tact. Failure to cope with this sort of thing is often the underlying cause of an executive's wanting or being asked to move on, and while one's natural reaction in such a situation is to blame the unreasonableness of others there are usually lessons to be learned for oneself.

Job satisfaction

If you're not in it for the fun, what the hell are you doing here anyway? So asks the author of that engagingly outrageous book *Up the Organisation*, by way of saying that job satisfaction is a vital factor in doing anything well and successfully. So look back over the jobs you have done and decide which activities have given you the most satisfaction and which the least. It need not have been the total job you found interesting; it may have been one assignment, such as planning a new system of distribution, writing a set of sales brochures, or determining the lay-out of a production process. Now that you have got several years of work experience it is relatively easy to discern a pattern and to work out its implications for your full-time occupation. This is very difficult for the 21-year-old to do — which is why so many go off course in the early days of their careers.

Leisure
Your leisure activities will also give you valuable clues to the source of job satisfaction. The reason why any vocational guidance test battery will include an interest questionnaire is that where it is possible to combine a deep interest with a job activity, the performance of the individual concerned will invariably be high.

It is, of course, only the fortunate minority who can combine their job with an abiding private interest. For most people, such pursuits as sport, music, drama, painting or simply pottering about with the family are a necessary relief from their working life. On the other hand, there is the phenomenon that although the broad mass of the working population are enjoying more leisure than ever before, executives are actually having to work harder and under greater pressure. Whether it is a healthy thing or not, either from the individual's point of view or from that of his firm, the tendency is for senior, highly-paid jobs to involve long hours and often work over weekends. Are you prepared to make this sacrifice? Are your wife and family? Leisure and time spent with your family will have a certain value to you; and if you don't budget for it, you may overlook a vital physical and psychological need.

What are the limiting factors?

At this stage it is easy to get carried away by what you could do — in theory. But by the time most people have passed their mid-30s they will have acquired commitments that are bound to limit their freedom of action.

Financial commitments
Whatever your financial package it will almost certainly be inadequate! There's some kind of Parkinson's Law by which expenditure always rises to meet one's income. But what are your true financial commitments? There are some expenses

you cannot easily get away from, those that you have become accustomed to but are not real necessities, and those which are sheer luxuries. These will no doubt be influenced by your life-style values. To some a sports or social club is essential; others like to entertain a lot; others again prefer to spend money on educational holidays or to educate their children privately. A change of job may increase or decrease expenditure — standard of clothing, cost of travel to work, cost of lunches or other essential costs. You may not have the capital to contemplate moving house unless you can get a bridging loan.

Family considerations

These days the careers of others in the family or the wish not to upset the children's education feature significantly in any job change. Who can change job more easily — the husband or the wife? With increasing opportunities for women this is no longer the foregone conclusion it was. Moreover, upsetting the whole friendship patterns of the family and local social and sports affiliations may be a greater price to pay than, say, a longer daily trip to work. Besides, a higher level job may involve a lot of home entertaining; is this possible in your present house and acceptable to your spouse?

Location

The restraints mentioned above are partly those of location, and in these days of easier travel and social mobility people are more ready to relocate than ever before. Apart from the cost of moving house — which is a very serious consideration, especially if it entails moving from the provinces to London — a new executive job may mean moving abroad or to a different part of the country. There is a growing band of executives who commute weekly from the continent and others who work abroad on a bachelor basis who prefer this to moving house. However, not every family can cope with this degree of separation, and then the area of job search must be much more restricted.

Identifying a course of action

Look back over the jobs you have done and decide which activities have given you the most satisfaction and which the least. Consider the role you tend to take in work and social situations, and review your leisure interests. Now draw the threads of these together and you will have an area of preferred activity and the type of role you are the most likely to play in it successfully. This can only be in generalised terms as yet; you know what you want from a job and how to evaluate jobs as they come along. Your 'needs matrix', as well as clearing your mind and helping you to get your priorities in perspective, will provide answers to these difficult questions: 'What is the minimum salary you are prepared to accept?' or 'What salary level are you looking for?' 'Where would you be prepared to work?' 'Are you prepared to go abroad?' 'What will the reaction of your family be if you are away from home for up to three weeks at a time?' 'How mobile are you?' The point we want to make is this: if you have thought out the implications of these questions in advance you will be better able to answer them and to answer them positively and with conviction. Not only will this impress the interviewer, who will feel you are a person who has faced up to reality and is making the best possible use of a difficult situation, but also it means you are no longer a hostage to fate; you are in command of your destiny.

A self-assessment test

This section, and the questions about yourself which it asks you to answer, will help you to rate yourself as objectively as a potential employer or personnel consultant might do. It will also serve to clarify some of your attitudes towards such matters as the importance you attach to such things as status and money. Thus it will help you to complete application blanks and prepare yourself for those questions that are sometimes difficult to answer off the cuff in interviews.

1. Attainments
The high spots of what you have achieved so far. For simplicity we look at these from three different angles.

☐ Academic — educational qualifications; grades.
☐ Professional — range and depth of your job knowledge and experience.
☐ Leadership — whom you have led and in what circumstances you were chosen.

ACADEMIC

Highest formal exams passed (school, college/university or private study) to map academic strengths and weaknesses:

Exam ....
Subjects taken........
Grades awarded ....

Now list your two best and two weakest subjects at each stage of your formal education. Do the same thing for any subjects you have taken by private study and for any courses you have taken.

PROFESSIONAL

List the principal aspects of your job as it is generally prac-tised (eg if you are a chief executive, this might include such matters as an acquaintance with accounting techniques, pro-duction technology, marketing, computer applications, etc) and grade your knowledge as follows:

0 — no experience
1 — casual or second-hand experience
2 — some experience/knowledge (would need help or have to read up to perform satisfactorily)
3 — good experience in the past, but out of date now
4 — competent
5 — expert

LEADERSHIP

☐ *By appointment*   *Role*
School   ....
College/university   ....
Armed services   ....
Other organisations   ....
At work   ....

☐ *By consent or election*
School   ....
College/university   ....
Other organisations   ....
At work   ....

☐ *Which category most applies to you?*
— Tend to be a leader in most situations
                    in formal situations only (by appointment)
                    in informal situations only (by election)
— Reluctant to exercise leadership function when appointed or elected
— Tend to take a 'number two' role
— No leadership experience worth mentioning

2. Basic aptitudes

We all have our own way of solving problems — the politician manipulates people, ie he gets somebody else to do the work for him; the salesman talks his way through (or out of) trouble; the engineer resorts to paper and drawing board; the craftsman to his work-bench. It is important to recognise our own basic aptitudes — or the lack of them. Rate your own basic aptitudes from the following list by awarding yourself 6 for the highest to 1 for the lowest and — for any aptitudes you simply do not possess.

☐ *Verbal* (a) Spoken: you follow arguments easily; can argue or negotiate persuasively and skilfully; have a large vocabulary; people listen to you. (b) Written: you read quickly; communicate well on paper; enjoy writing reports; have a large vocabulary.

☐ *Numerical* You are happiest when working with figures or formulae; resort to a slide-rule or use stats whenever feasible; fill your reports with figures and argue from quantifiable 'facts'.

☐ *Practical* (a) You resort to pencil and paper sketches/diagrams whenever you can; can think in three dimensions; (b) You like to work with things or go down to the shop floor to work things out; prefer to tackle down-to-earth 'real' problems rather than to speculate on theoretical possibilities.

☐ *Creative* You enjoy playing with ideas, testing hypotheses, and coming up with novel solutions (even if impractical); the 'status quo' frustrates you and you are always trying to change the system; may be inventive or artistic.

☐ *Methodical* Everything you do is neatly set out — home, workshop, office files and drawers, etc; you rarely make careless mistakes in calculations or grammar; have a good memory for facts and figures; are a great one for law, order and method.

☐ *People-oriented* You are a facilitator, fixer or coordinator; work through people — you marshall your resources for them to solve your problems; are good at persuading people, influencing them and working up support for or against an issue; have a way with people that tends to command their allegiance.

3. Interests and hobbies

Most of us cherish the hope of pursuing some interest or

other 'if only we could find the time to get around to it', for instance writing or painting. But if in practice you have never found the leisure time to devote to your pipe dream then you probably have no deep motivation to develop it further. However, if there are any hobbies or interests that you are actively involved in, put them down. They may have considerable occupational significance, particularly if they highlight talents that you are not able to employ in your job.

Interest	Time spent per week	Rank order
Helping people (eg voluntary social work)	. . . .	. . . .
Persuading people (eg local politics, lecturing)	. . . .	. . . .
Experimenting with words or ideas (eg writing, Open University study)	. . . .	. . . .
Scientific or mathematical	. . . .	. . . .
Developing manual or technical skills (eg carpentry, photography)	. . . .	. . . .
The arts (music, painting, etc)	. . . .	. . . .
Outdoor activities and sports	. . . .	. . . .
Collecting (antiques, etc)	. . . .	. . . .
Others	. . . .	. . . .

4. Personality

We all have persistent personality traits which enable other people to predict how we are likely to act or react to certain 'typical' life or social situations. It is these persistent traits that you should concentrate on here. Base your conclusions on how you have in reality reacted in the past, not on how you might have acted if things had been different!

In career guidance, psychologists concentrate on four main traits:

    (a) sociable v self-contained
    (b) phlegmatic v excitable
    (c) tough-minded v sensitive
    (d) conforming v independent.

In each of the following there are five possible reactions. Read each pair, ask yourself which reaction applies to you, and tick only those that do. When you have done this add up your scores on sides A and B and subtract one from the other to give a positive score. If the final score in any category is less than 3 this particular trait is not significant for you. Make a note of a score above 3, and finally check conclusions with a friend to avoid bias.

(a) ARE YOU SOCIABLE OR SELF-CONTAINED?

A	B
☐ Lively and talkative	☐ Quiet and subdued
☐ Warm-hearted and sociable	☐ Shy and self-contained
☐ Adventurous, welcome new situations and challenges	☐ Conservative (with a small c), dislike fresh challenges or changes
☐ Impulsive, quickly change plans	☐ Controlled, only change plans after thinking them through carefully
☐ Easy-going, have many friends	☐ Serious, with a few deep friendships

If your score on A is higher than on B then you are sociable; if B is higher than A you are self-contained. If your scores balance out then this trait is not significant for you.

(b) ARE YOU PHLEGMATIC OR EXCITABLE?

A	B
☐ Patient, willing to wait	☐ Impatient, want to do things straight away
☐ Placid, not easily upset	☐ Anxious, easily upset
☐ Careful, concerned to make good	☐ Careless, not very concerned about the impression made on others
☐ Relaxed	☐ Tense and restless
☐ Slow to be roused to activity	☐ Quickly aroused to activity

Score as above. Caution: it is easy to draw moral conclusions from your answers here. The fact that you are inclined to be anxious and careless does not mean that you are necessarily irresponsible or cannot be depended upon. But it may well mean that you have to overcompensate for these tendencies and that a stressful job or situation will make heavier demands on you psychologically than it will on others.

(c) ARE YOU TOUGH-MINDED OR SENSITIVE?

A	B
☐ Practical and realistic	☐ Imaginative
☐ Enjoy rough activities	☐ Avoid rough activities
☐ Prefer to do things yourself	☐ Seek and welcome help from others
☐ Appear hard and tough to others	☐ Appear soft and gentle to others
☐ Dislike emotion and sentiment	☐ Welcome expressions of emotion or expressions of feelings

Score as above. Caution: in our society sensitivity is associated with femininity and toughness with masculinity and there are cultural pressures to reinforce this from infancy. In practice, the reverse is often true.

(d) ARE YOU CONFORMING OR INDEPENDENT?

A	B
☐ Welcome direction and advice	☐ Resent 'interference' and advice
☐ Submissive, go along with friends' or colleagues' suggestions	☐ Assertive, like to get your own way
☐ Prefer conventional and traditional ideas	☐ Radical, welcome change and go out to achieve it for its own sake
☐ Conscientious, keep to the rules	☐ Prepared to break the rules if it suits your purpose
☐ Follow the beliefs of others and accept their attitudes	☐ Prefer to make up your own mind and disbelieve if not convinced

Score as above.

Your personal profile

1. ATTAINMENTS (from pp 49-50)

(a) Academic
Your highest scholastic achievement:
at school . . . .
at college/university . . . .
private study . . . .

(b) Professional
Summary from p 50.

(c) Leadership
Most significant attainments from p 50.

2. BASIC APTITUDES
Tick the following as appropriate from your answers on p 51:

☐ Verbal
☐ Numerical
☐ Practical

☐ Creative
☐ Methodical
☐ People-oriented

3. INTERESTS AND HOBBIES
Record your conclusions from pp 51-52.

4. PERSONALITY
Tick as appropriate and record positive scores.

☐ Sociable
☐ Phlegmatic
☐ Tough-minded
☐ Conforming

☐ Self-contained
☐ Excitable
☐ Sensitive
☐ Independent

What are you best equipped to do?

Most people are able to do quite a number of different jobs, largely depending on the opportunities presented to them and on the society in which they live. The more intelligent you are and the wider your range of interests, the wider your range of choice. Nevertheless you are likely to derive a greater satisfaction from jobs which most nearly match the profile of academic attainment, aptitudes, interests and personality which you have now built up.

Assuming that you are over 35 — or at least over 30 — many of the options open to you earlier will now have gone or be too costly to attain owing to family responsibilities or lack of money. If you wish to make a change, review the alternatives in a logical way concentrating on your strengths and being aware of your weaknesses. Consider the activity, the level and the environment of the work you have done and of the possible openings to you. Try to change only one variable; to attempt more may be too heavily demanding psychologically.

Activity This may be the time to improve your qualifications and thus specialise in an aspect of your work that especially interests you. The salesman may decide to come inside and become a buyer; the production engineer, a tester or maintenance engineer; the researcher, a teacher or trainer.

Level Broadly, you have the choice of coasting along at your present level or of climbing the ladder; to step backwards is very difficult — unless you break right away. If you wish to climb you must be very realistic when assessing your abilities.

In many instances it will demand further study, perhaps higher qualifications, and make very heavy demands on your time and on you personally. By all means realise your full potential but don't overreach yourself. The solution for you may be to be a bigger fish in a smaller pond or to take a senior staff job with no departmental responsibilities.

Environment The environment within which you have worked may, on reflection, be more important to you than the actual work you do, or vice versa. We are all familiar with the problems created by a change at the top, especially after a takeover or merger. Try to match the new environment with your own personality and think hard and long before making a fundamental change.

Obviously, within the confines of this book, it would be impossible and grossly misleading to attempt to guide each individual reader towards a specific career change. What we can do, however, is to help you to match yourself with the career profiles of successful people in broad occupational areas or 'career types'. If, to a substantial extent, your profile does not match the job you are in, then you should seriously consider making a change by transfer to another department or activity or leaving the company for a more challenging or congenial environment. If that change would involve upsetting more than one of the three variables — work activity, level or environment — then we strongly suggest that you seek professional guidance from one of the bodies listed in Appendix E.

Career types

Executive/decision-making
You enjoy running things and taking policy decisions; you are interested in broad issues and the interpretation of data prepared by others.

☐ Academic: any subject, preferably at pass degree level as a minimum.

☐ Professional: rate four or five in at least 50 per cent of the relevant areas of job knowledge.

☐ Leadership: tend to lead in most situations. Lots of initiative.

☐ Aptitude: verbal/numerical and people-oriented.

☐ Strongest interests: competitive activities, social organisations.

☐ Personality: self-contained, tough-minded, independent.

Jobs to consider: running an operation or part of an operation, carrying profit- or other objective-attaining responsibility.

Administrative

You tend to be strongest in the following:

☐ Academic: languages, social studies or science; tend to have performed well in exams.
☐ Professional: likely to be fully qualified but not 'brilliant'.
☐ Leadership: like responsibility, but prefer number two role.
☐ Aptitude: methodical, verbal (b) or numerical.
☐ Strongest interests: working with figures, words or ideas.
☐ Outdoor, active.
☐ Personality: self-contained, phlegmatic, conforming.

Jobs to consider: company secretary, local government, Civil Service, consultancy.

Altruistic

As the word implies, you enjoy work that involves helping others, with financial gain as a secondary consideration.

☐ Academic: languages or social studies.
☐ Professional: may have background in personnel or some other people-oriented function.
☐ Leadership: social organisations, eg local politics, church activities.
☐ Leisure: involves voluntary social work, eg marriage guidance.
☐ Aptitude: verbal or people-oriented.
☐ Strongest interests: helping people or organising; words and ideas.
☐ Personality: sociable, excitable, sensitive.

Jobs to consider: social work, religious and charity administration, nursing, social reform organisation, politics.

Artistic

You enjoy work that involves creativity or inventiveness (by doing or appreciation).

☐ Academic: languages, art or craft subjects.
☐ Professional: may not have bothered to qualify.
☐ Leadership: good in situations that require initiative and persistence.
☐ Interests: artistic or craft skills.
☐ Aptitude: creative.
☐ Strongest interests: the arts, working with materials or tools, persuading people.
☐ Personality: self-contained, excitable, independent.

Jobs to consider: setting up on one's own to fulfil the growing demand for craftsman-made, 'one-off' objects that big organisations no longer supply, eg cabinet-making, metalwork, restoring antiques or pictures, etc.

Literary
You like working with words, ideas and feelings.

☐ Academic: languages or social studies.
☐ Professional: probably good professional qualifications.
☐ Leadership: unimportant.
☐ Leisure: writing and serious reading.
☐ Aptitude: verbal or creative.
☐ Strongest interests: words and ideas, the arts, persuading people.
☐ Personality: sociable, excitable, independent.

Jobs to consider: technical writer, librarian, information or communication specialist (in company). Possibly writing — though, as with all the arts, you have to achieve a very high standard to earn a living!

Persuasive
You enjoy work which influences others towards a course of action. This may involve getting them to buy something or, in another sphere, bringing them together for the purposes of an organisation.

☐ Academic: languages, the arts or social studies.
☐ Professional: possibly no formal qualifications.
☐ Leadership: elective leadership, especially where initiative and persistence required.
☐ Leisure: will have taken part in money-raising (eg school or club funds), voluntary PR or organising social events.

☐ Aptitude: people-oriented, verbal.
☐ Strongest interests: words or ideas, competitive sports.
☐ Personality: sociable, tough-minded, independent.

Jobs to consider: advertising, public relations, sales and marketing, fund-raising organisation consultant, personnel officer, full-time club secretary.

Practical

You would enjoy a skilled job that involves working with your hands.

☐ Academic: practical subjects.
☐ Professional: craft or technical qualifications and training.
☐ Leadership: not important but might have been a formally appointed supervisor.
☐ Leisure: do-it-yourself, especially working with raw materials rather than ready-made kits.
☐ Aptitude: practical.
☐ Strongest interests: working with materials, the arts, helping people with practical projects.
☐ Personality: phlegmatic, sensitive, conforming.

Jobs to consider: working in a laboratory in a skilled capacity, owning a garage or repair workshop; skilled building crafts or home-improvement franchise.

Scientific

You have a basic curiosity and interest in how and why things happen.

☐ Academic: scientific or mathematical subjects.
☐ Professional: academic rather than technical qualifications, possibly involving subjects pursued for their own sake rather than for their possible commercial applications.
☐ Leadership: small group leadership (by election or consent).
☐ Leisure: some private work of observation of a scientific nature.
☐ Aptitude: numerical.
☐ Strongest interests: working with tools or materials, science, music.
☐ Personality: self-contained, phlegmatic, independent.

Jobs to consider: teaching at secondary or tertiary level,

research and development in industry, working with computers.

Technical/technological
You enjoy work in an environment where tools and machinery are involved.

☐ Academic: technical, scientific or mathematical subjects.
☐ Professional: as above.
☐ Leadership: not an important factor.
☐ Leisure: enjoyment of hobbies or do-it-yourself pursuits that involve tinkering with machinery.
☐ Aptitude: practical, methodical or numerical.
☐ Strongest interests: working with tools, following developments in technology, active outdoor pursuits.
☐ Personality; phlegmatic, tough-minded, conforming.

Jobs to consider: technical college teaching, the production side in industry.

4. Planning a Job Strategy

Now is the time to bring all your business experience and expertise to bear on the most challenging and important assignment you have ever tackled — setting out to find a new executive job for yourself. The first essential is to be systematic and to operate in a planned way: as you would do if you were tackling any other kind of business operation. The stages are:

1. set up a job file;
2. carry out a survey of the total market;
3. set your objectives against a timescale;
4. set an interview-getting strategy.

This may sound very elementary to you, but it is surprising how few people get off on the right foot. The best way to make sure that you do so is to open a job file.

1. Job file

In this file you will put everything appertaining to your search — a progress chart, your self-analysis, live applications, dead applications, personal contacts.

Progress chart
On a piece of white card (card because it will be handled a lot) enter these headings — Company, Job, Salary, Location, Initial enquiry, Application sent, Progress. Divide the last section into six narrow vertical columns (for dates) and allow space for your written comments. Check this card daily and always keep it completely up to date. As jobs fall through run a thin red line through the entry.

Behind this card keep a series of 'call reports' — that is,

fuller notes for your future guidance of the names of people met at interview; and difficulties encountered such as questions which bowled you out, deficiencies pointed out, any mistakes you think you might have made and points that were especially well received. Do a call report for every application that goes beyond the interview stage.

You will also need to keep a note of your investigations into companies. This will include extracts from reference books, newspaper cuttings, some of their current ads (job and product), any financial information you can obtain, etc. (See below for some guidelines on company investigations.) Where you keep this information is a matter of choice, but as it is possible to use it more than once we suggest you keep it in the progress chart section.

Self-analysis
This section will contain all your notes from Chapter 3. Keep your summary and objectives on the top for ease of reference, together with a copy of your summary cv (see Chapter 8). As you go along you will want to modify or expand some points so be sure to keep your summary and objectives right up to date. It is probably less cumbersome to enter alterations in the section concerned even if it does look untidy!

Live applications
Number these and keep a reference index at the front. As jobs fall through (sorry, but one must be realistic!) delete them from the list. It is easier to keep these in date order — as your progress chart. Every communication with a prospective employer should be recorded — phone calls and the outcome of them, correspondence and a summary of your reply or a copy if typed, and finally a note of any reason that may have been offered for turning you down. Keep the original advertisement, or an introductory note, on top for ready reference.

Dead applications
As soon as applications fall through remove them to the dead section so as not to clutter the live file and, if this section becomes too long, open another dead file. It is worth keeping these old papers as a job may suddenly fall vacant again or a similar one arise with the same company. Also they will be useful for study if you persistently seem to fail to get beyond

the interview stage. There may be something wrong with your letter-writing technique which a friend will be able to point out to you.

Personal contacts

Keep a list of the names of all your useful contacts together with their addresses and phone numbers. Alongside each name make a note of when you were last in contact and for what purpose. Keep these in alphabetical order, as far as possible, for rapid reference if one of them phones. It is worth keeping a similar note of the people you meet at interviews or are in correspondence with. Some people find it easier to keep such names in alphabetical order in a book or a card index.

2. Surveying the market

If you have carried out the steps in the last chapter you will have a clear idea of the direction you want to go and of your priorities. At this stage it can only be in general terms; if it is too specific you will probably have leapt to too hasty a conclusion and may well spend too long tackling too narrow a field. Make sure that you survey the field as widely as possible and with as few preconceived notions as possible. Study the *Financial Times* and *The Economist*; examine the economic forecasts of the CBI, the Economist Intelligence Unit, the business schools, the Henley Forecasting Centre, OECD and EEC analyses and predictions; read *The Director, Management Today* and your own professional press; talk to friends 'in the know'. You will quickly begin to see how the land lies and gain a shrewd idea of the state of the employment market, of salary levels, of industries and firms on the rise and those in decline. You will also soon get a feel of technological developments and will draw conclusions on likely future trends in the shorter term. The more informed opinion you can obtain the better. Undoubtedly you will need to 'polish your crystal ball' if you want to see very far ahead but on the whole things move slowly and the five-to-ten year trend is discernible. At interviews later you will be able constantly to refine your views and check your conclusions — which will have the added advantage of impressing your interviewer with the depth of your knowledge.

The kind of broad trend you might think about and which you can build up a picture of by reading and discussion is, for example, how the discovery of North Sea oil affects the pattern of British industry and what opportunities it creates.

The big executive job market that has developed in the mid and later 70s, of course, is in the primary producing countries — notably in the oil-rich Middle East. Almost literally, they have all the money in the world, but an acute shortage of trained manpower to run the infrastructure of industrial, engineering, construction and commercial development that has accompanied the oil price boom. Working and living conditions are tough but opportunities (and salaries) for executives with any kind of technological skill and experience are considerable, as a glance at the recruitment pages in the press will show — and there are now signs of a demand for more general managerial expertise, particularly in the financial and marketing spheres. This seems likely to grow in the wake of a more settled prosperity following on the hectic years of the initial oil boom.

Back in the UK there has been little let-up in legislation — explicit or in the form of guidelines — in the field of industrial relations. Even medium-sized companies now need people with specialised knowledge of employment law to deal with increasingly sophisticated and well-prepared shop-floor and white-collar negotiators. A training course in industrial relations at a polytechnic could be an excellent investment if your aptitudes are verbal and people-oriented. If, on the other hand, they run more towards numerical and logical skills, then the potential of the 'new technology' is almost endless. Enormous changes in production, marketing and communication methods are already over the horizon, and the implications of the microchip and its associated technology across the whole field of business and industry are beginning to be realised. No one quite knows yet what the effects will be but it is pretty certain that they will change radically where and how we will live and work. There will be periods, like the present one, when the future is far from clear — but also lots of opportunities for those who are lucky enough to have the right qualifications or the right kind of intelligence, and for those who can recognise the opportunities that will occur.

Job advertisements, in fact, are themselves one of the most valuable sources of information — not only those in your own area of expertise but in general. It is said that the advertisements of the selection consultants are read avidly in top financial circles because these so often presage other developments, or are the first indications the outside world has of important changes at the top. So it will pay you to see which companies are recruiting and which are not. In some cases the jobs advertised will clearly be replacements, but others will follow a typical development pattern, viz investment in research is reflected within a year in design and development; this leads to a build-up in production; which in turn leads to growth in the sales force. Admittedly, this is on a fairly long timescale, but by discerning such a trend you can see which firms are going ahead and where vacancies are likely to arise and in which functions. Another thing to watch is the salary and man specifications. They must be studied together. If certain skills are in short supply then man specifications are loosened (ie men with poorer qualifications and less experience are accepted) and salaries raised to attract new people to the industry. The MSL Index, published quarterly and usually commented on in the press in some detail, gives moving totals of demand by function together with a commentary on the state of the market. This is done by a systematic analysis of all advertisements for posts carrying a certain minimum salary of seniority. By comparing one month with another, patterns can easily be discerned. From this you can soon see which categories are in demand and which in recession, salary levels, the type of people sought, age bands, and where most jobs are advertised at the salary levels you are interested in.

So to sum up you will now know:

(a) the broad economic trends;
(b) trends in technology;
(c) the overall state of the job market;
(d) the state of development or retrenchment in individual firms;
(e) the demand position in your own function or area of interest.

You are in a position, therefore, to go back to your career aims and match these to areas of opportunity in the market. You can decide in which direction to launch yourself, and you will also have a pretty shrewd idea of the comparative difficulty of finding a suitable vacancy and whether or not to modify your 'asking price'.

3. Setting your objectives

As you will know, the more advanced managements don't muddle along in the pious hope of increasing profit each year (or maintaining dividends); they plan ahead and set themselves quantified objectives and then ensure that the organisation is right and people well motivated to achieve these objectives within a given timescale. In your case the longer-term objective is to get a job that will satisfy as many of your needs as possible; and the shorter-term aim is to get interviews. The first fact you have to face is that the higher up the organisation you have been, the higher your salary, and the greater your age, the longer it will take you to get a job. That is why senior executives are given larger golden handshakes. Many factors affect this. The main ones are:

(a) It scarcely matters how expert you are in your own field or how well known; the hard fact is that there will be few vacancies at any one time for men like you.

(b) The job-filling process at senior levels is a slow one. The specialist selection consultants reckon on six weeks from initial briefing to making an offer as the very minimum. With overseas appointments six months or more is quite common; 'official' appointments will be somewhere in between. It is extremely unlikely that you will walk straight into a job — though we hope you will — and if you receive a firm offer in the early days you should consider very carefully before turning it down and playing hard to get — because you will be in the lucky top five per cent.

The timescale of probability
As a rule of thumb the very minimum time (for that lucky five per cent) will be one month. Add to this the period of notice you have to give if you are already in employment; if you have been warned of impending redundancy you may be released earlier (unless a company is being kept going until the last possible moment in which case you may be offered a premium or the size of your handshake may depend on whether you stay until the bitter end). Add to this another

month for each five years over 35 and another month for each £1000 above £8000 pa. So the 39-year-old aiming at £9000 plus (essential minimum) is likely to take at least three months; the 46-year-old aiming at £12,000 plus — seven months; the 52-year-old £15,000 pa man — well over 12 months. If you are unlucky or become redundant at a time when the recruitment market is slack (especially June-August, November-December) it may well take even longer. So if you decide to go into business on your own account by investing your golden handshake in a pub or a chain of holiday cottages the sooner you get started the better. Keep this timescale of probability firmly in mind (write it beneath your aims and objectives inside your job file; it will reassure you when you receive the 20th or 200th refusal). On the other hand don't let it lull you into a false sense of security. It doesn't mean that in six months' time the right job will turn up; it means that if you market yourself effectively with sustained effort, within six months the probability is that you will have found a suitable appointment.

How long can you afford to wait?
This is the second critical parameter to take into account. If you are in employment this is no problem; if not you may be forced to take some early, drastic action.

(a) If you limit your area of choice too strictly (so as not to upset the children's schooling) this will probably delay things even more.

(b) You must market yourself correctly and at the right price. It will be better to drop that extra £1000 right from the start rather than stick out for the extra. After all £1000 is only one month's salary at £12,000 pa and the capital you will spend during the month that you are out of work represents many months of hard saving. The hard and apparently unfair fact is that the longer you are out of work the more difficult it will be to persuade an employer that there is nothing wrong with you! Ask any selection consultant; and wouldn't you yourself have said the same in the past? Unless you have vast financial resources or are in a job it is not advisable to play hard to get.

Naming your price

Equally it means don't underprice yourself unrealistically. The £10,000 pa man who is prepared to accept a senior lecturer's salary of around £8000 is one thing; but to apply for a job in his old function at £8000 and with a much lower status is quite another. 'Why is this man prepared to drop so much? He must be desperate' (and by implication useless) — 'I know he says he is quite prepared to take a drop but how long will he stay once the market improves?' — 'Oh yes he's well qualified all right; too well qualified to be satisfied with this job — [aside] I'd have to watch out for my job if he were appointed.' And so on. You've probably heard this sort of thing said.

So how do you fix your price? This will depend on several factors:

(a) whether you are in employment;
(b) whether you wish to stay in the same activity or function;
(c) whether the type of job you are now going for has an entirely different salary structure.

It could well be that you would quote a different price to different employers. If it's a choice between an inherent risk in a new consultancy, a secure post in government, and a lectureship (with the expectation of additional income from freelance consultancy) you could well be prepared to accept £12,500, £10,000 and £8000 respectively, as it is possible to adjust your life accordingly. To get a feel of current salaries find out your current salary scale, study the job advertisements in the press, and look out for commentaries on salary levels by such firms as Hay-MSL and AIC (but be wary of those based on what candidates would like as they are always on the high side). Depending on the strength of your own position draw up your own upper, median and lower quartiles. If you are in a job and are prepared to go to a competitor aim for the upper quartile (he will expect to pay it); or a median salary if you are aiming for a promotion; if you are changing completely aim for the lower quartile. If you are redundant and can afford to wait, aim for the median but don't be too rigid about it. If you are close to the dole fix yourself at the lower quartile 'bargain' price — after all you are unlikely to stay at the bottom for long if you are any good. When an employer decides he wants you he may well offer you a little more even on a fixed scale; this is certainly so with teaching and Civil Service appointments – providing that you justify it, of course. If you decide on a complete change then you will have to take the rate for the job. The person who has made a first career in the Armed Services usually has a very realistic view today of his value to a civilian organisation, and is frequently both more ready to start at the bottom and more adaptable than his industrial counterparts – especially those who have been made redundant.

At the time of writing (1981) salary levels are particularly variable – even within the same industry and irrespective of levels of profitability. This reflects the fact that in firms without a clearly thought out salary policy, the pay situation has in recent years been in more than usual disarray. Some firms, for instance, held back salaries at upper levels in line with Government policy in 1976-78 and some did not; others found ways around Government directives by increasing perks, so that a salary structure which looks to be less than the going rate is in fact in line with it. In other and more recent cases, there are firms which have managed to hold back wage demands in the recession and others which have been less successful in so doing. This again would be echoed in levels of executive remuneration. Another factor is the difference in the cost of housing in various parts of the country – some employers recognise this by paying a London weighting, others do not or do so to varying degrees. The upshot is that a similarly described job may carry a salary of £25,000 in London, but only £16,000 to £18,000 in the provinces. Thus, in a buyer's market you may have to take a lower salary to come in at the same level as you were in before with another company. Employers tend to be suspicious of people who are prepared to take a drop in salary, but in present circumstances you may have a very good reason to do so which you should be prepared to outline at an interview.

4. An interview-getting strategy

By now you have decided on the type of job you are aiming for, you have fixed a timescale and you have set an offer price bracket and are ready for the launch.

You need not feel, however, that you are now entirely on your own; there are other forces you can deploy to your advantage at each stage of your job-getting campaign. Timing will depend on your judgement and the strength of your need (see Chapter 7). Likewise, the length of time between each phase of your search will depend on the 'timescale of necessity'.

Phase 1. The publicity, test marketing phase

A new product will not sell until it is known to be on offer. So the first essential step is to make sure that the people who are most likely to be able to help you are aware that you are on the market and what your preferences are. This will include your personal contacts, executive search and selection consultancies. If you are in a job this can present problems. You will need to be very discreet as there have been cases of executives being sacked for disloyalty when it has been discovered that they are 'looking around'. The higher up the ladder you are the more important discretion becomes because of possible effects on the stock market. How you declare your availability will depend on your status, salary level, occupation, and the attitude of your present employer.

Phase 2. Study the ads

At all levels this will follow closely on phase 1. It is vital that you do not let up your efforts until you have a confirmed offer in your hand. This is the ad-watching stage. To save you looking at every publication and reading every ad there are certain useful guidelines. Few jobs over £7000 a year appear in the local press. Few jobs over £8500 will appear in the regional press *alone*. Most managerial appointments appear in the quality daily and weekend press though increasingly their monopoly is being challenged by the more popular press. Other publications, notably *The Economist* and the *Financial Times*, carry a wide range of managerial appointments. At this stage we suggest that you go to your local library and scan all these for at least a week to get a feel of the market you are particularly interested in and to mark which days are the most popular for advertising (traditionally Monday and Saturday are poor days). Then you can pick out the most promising dailies and Sundays and study them *every* day. If you have capital to invest then you must add the *FT* to your list.

The evening papers are also mostly of use only at the under £7000 level. Another rule of thumb is to read only your own professional column and the management and executive column in lineage and then study the display columns (and some of these are classified too). There are separate pages for public and official appointments. The consultancy firms usually advertise on set days — Wednesday, Thursday and Friday being the most popular.

The next must is the journal of your own profession. These vary enormously but in, for example, medicine, law and architecture some 90 per cent of all job ads for the professions are contained in one or two professional journals. In personnel management some 60 per cent appear only in the official journal. At times of mounting executive redundancy, companies will tend to place the bulk of their advertising for jobs in the main professional journals, thus saving considerable sums. We suggest that you start by looking through back numbers — remember it can take three months to fill a job and the application list is usually kept open until the last moment (except with official appointments). Follow up urgently anything that interests you, preferably by phone. At this stage it will pay you to be fairly selective. Go for the jobs you really want and apply to them first and leave the others to one side for a week or two. Cut out the ads and mount them in your job file and record action taken.

Phase 3. The cold canvass
If Phases 1 and 2 are patently not producing results, or if a shortage of funds demands more drastic action, you should start thinking in terms of the cold canvass. Choose your firms carefully, or else you will end up with a large duplicating and postage bill and find yourself sending out 1000 letters! The most useful way to set about it is:

1. Study the information provided in the standard works of reference which are listed in Appendix D. These provide a wealth of data on who manufactures what and where, on company policies and plans and, in some cases, on future developments.
2. Read the financial and business press regularly. It will give you an up-to-the-minute picture of which firms are expanding and in what directions — both in terms of activities and geographically. Try to spot their needs

71

for someone like yourself *before* they advertise. This is not as difficult as it might sound. For example, a new factory will require executive staff to man it or to replace others who are withdrawn from elsewhere in the company; a merger/takeover may well mean openings for men with big company experience or men to replace an ageing and ailing management team; the introduction of a new product, the receipt of a very large order or the replacement of a computer will all probably call for additional staff, some at relatively senior levels; the appointment of Mr X may mean a reshuffle of the entire management team and the introduction of a new style of management, and so on. Admittedly this is more useful at the junior to middle management levels (top management will have been decided in advance) but it is not always so. Very frequently companies fail to realise the scope for a good man or the contribution he could make until they are confronted with one who can spell out the details for them and they have physically seen him. Some guidance on writing 'on spec' letters is given in Appendix A. But you have to face the fact that although a far-sighted management will make the job to fit the man, relatively few come into this category — so be prepared for a vast number of rejections!

Registers and placement agencies

A list of such agencies — there are not very many — is given in Appendix E. Placement agencies will see you, evaluate you, give you advice and place your name on their register if they think they can help you. It must, however, be remembered that these people are in business to fill jobs — not to offer careers counselling as such — and they will only interview you if they think there is a strong chance of placing you in a specific job. They offer no miracles or instant solutions, as the people who run them will readily admit. If you are outstandingly good in your field, the executive placement agencies can be very useful — but then you may not have much trouble anyway. In short, they are one of the many tools at your disposal.

Executive counselling services

A number of organisations were born during the early 1970s to cater for the needs of the redundant senior executives who needed general advice on how to present themselves in person, and perhaps more fundamental advice on making a career change. Those listed (see Appendix E) are known to have a good reputation (there may well be others). They frequently employ psychologists and trained career advisers as well as former senior business executives. Charges vary widely from up to £500 to £2000 or more. Essentially you buy advice and time. Don't pay more than you need to! Many recruitment consultants also give free advice to 'good' candidates (though they may not advertise this as a service — especially those with a 'talent-bank').

Advertising your availability

Should you advertise yourself? On the whole, the opinion is that, as far as the national press is concerned, this is highly unlikely to product results, unless you have capital to invest or would like to buy a directorship in a small firm. In that case you should clearly specify what you want and what you have to offer, for example:

> Return on £150,000 investment and energetic participation sought by experienced retail store executive. Reply to Box No 1234, *Daily Telegraph*.

The box number is a good idea, because it avoids calls at your home from the undesirable characters who unfortunately tend to be attracted by the notion of someone with money to invest.

The professional press is well worth using, if you have a specific qualification or skill that you can offer, for example:

> Distribution problems? Experienced physical distribution manager who has controlled both manual and automated systems for leading motor parts manufacturer available now. Box No 5678, *Commercial Motor*.

Advertising in professional or specialist journals is a lot cheaper than national newspapers, and you can pick with some precision the potential employers you are trying to reach.

Some professional journals are making special efforts to

73

help individuals advertise their availability for employment and are grouping such advertisements together to give them greater impact. For those who can command a salary above £15,000 and who are interested in Europe there is also a medium called International Classified Advertising. This is connected to an organisation which publishes a journal ten times a year and which will take display and lineage advertisements from subscribers. The subscription is £60 pa. Address: A Manley, International Executive Search Newsletter, 3 rue d'Hautville, 75010 Paris, France.

A job strategy for top, middle and junior management

Top management
Provided that you stay in your present function the personal contact at the club, by private letter (sent to a home address) or phone call (again from home) will soon get the ball rolling. A word with your financial advisers may well bear fruit — they may be able to put you in touch with company chairmen who need someone with your expertise but who for commercial reasons daren't say so openly until the deal is completed.

If it can be made public, a carefully worded press announcement containing some specific reference to what you have done, issued through your PR advisers, may help enormously, eg

> One of the casualties from the forthcoming merger between x and y will be John Smith, the Marketing Director of y and the man largely responsible for its growth from sales of £1 million four years ago to the forecast £5 million this year. I understand that he has already been offered several alternatives in the new organisation but feels that he would rather head up the function in a new and developing company. As a result of the merger company x's well-known market development procedures will be introduced throughout the group, giving little scope for an ideas man like John Smith. The changeover is not likely to be fully effective until the new year.

This type of announcement will probably lead to many offers and your name will be noted by all the executive search consultants (head-hunters). Any reputable management selection consultancy should also be approached. Some will see you; others will want particulars to keep on file; others will advise you to watch their advertisement columns — but they will all be interested to hear from you. A short note setting out what you are looking for accompanied by a well-set-out curriculum vitae will be quite sufficient; avoid filling out application blanks unnecessarily at this stage.

Middle management

If you are in the £8000 to £15,000 bracket you are probably not sufficiently well known to adopt the PR release approach and will need to use your personal contacts in a different way. To be brutal, it is less likely that you will be on first name terms with company chairmen and the company's City advisers. On the other hand, you may well have met a number of influential people who may be in a position to help you. Unless you are likely to command a salary in excess of £15,000 pa, the executive search consultants are not likely to be interested in you, but the management selection firms will be very glad to know you. If during the last three years you have met one of these consultants by all means contact him (by appointment so that he can look up your records). He may well be prepared to give you half an hour's free advice and perhaps circulate your papers among his colleagues. On the whole these companies do not keep lists of potential candidates and will advise you to 'watch their columns' — but they are always glad to hear from a person with a good record.

The last five years has seen the considerable rise of the 'out-placement agency' (see Chapter 7). Some of them work almost exclusively for employers, others for the public at large. The best of these will give you advice and help with most aspects of the job-getting process. Some will help you market yourself by sending your cv to selected employers and consultants. The marketing aspect needs to be looked at cautiously. Their cvs are easily identifiable so that all individuality is lost. Not all employers favour this approach and many will put them straight into the waste paper basket on the grounds that the executive who can't market himself is by definition no good at marketing a company. This is not entirely fair but it is a fact. Their marketing service is a soft — but by no means a cheap — option and in the opinion of the authors should be treated with extreme caution. The advice they give to help people to help themselves is another matter, as is their value as a well-screened register of possible candidates to the employer who is actively looking for people.

Junior management/professional men

Once again the personal contact may be useful. The executive search firm will not be interested and the selection consultants in general will only tell you to watch their columns. However, the specialist selection firms may well be able to help you — the computer, accountancy, marketing, advertising, personnel specialists spring to mind. This apart, advertising yourself is unlikely to be very useful as the hard fact is that you are unlikely to be well known or in especially short supply. The principal exception could be if you are known in your field as a writer or lecturer or are in the public eye. Here again, though, you will be able most probably to use personal contacts.

A final word

You will go through periods when you are full of optimism, and others of profound despair when the five jobs you were so optimistic about have fallen through and then nothing else seems to turn up for weeks. It is absolutely vital for your own morale and for your ultimate success that you maintain the pressure all the time. Don't delay unncessarily moving on to the next phase; maintain your daily study of the press; keep up your contacts, and above all don't give up.

It is at this stage that a good, honest friend who can help you to keep things in perspective and to see yourself objectively is especially valuable. Fundamental questions may need to be asked: is your self-assessment or reading of the market realistic? Are you attempting the impossible or being too narrow in your search? Are you panicking and putting people off by selling yourself too hard? Experience has shown that a high percentage of those who follow the guidance in this book succeed. If after three months you seem to be getting nowhere then seek advice and if necessary pay for it. Don't soldier on alone; two heads are invariably better than one.

AN OPENING TO MORE CAREERS.

Open The Daily Telegraph and you'll find more job opportunities than in any other national paper.

40% of all situations vacant that appear in the quality press appear in The Daily Telegraph.*

It opens the door to an exciting variety of career possibilities, in all fields and at all levels.

So it will help you on your way, both now and when you're more experienced.

Open one today and choose an opening for yourself.

The Daily Telegraph

*Source: M.E.A.L. January-December 1980

5. Making the Most of Your Contacts

Whenever opinions are canvassed about the most effective method of getting a job, personal contacts and introductions come up as the answer. Apart from internal promotion, more people get jobs through direct or indirect recommendations and leads from friends, acquaintances and colleagues than by any other means. This fact is borne out in a BIM report *Selecting Managers* which shows that only about 50 per cent of executive jobs are ever advertised openly. The majority are either filled by promotion or through personal contact. It is well known that when a new company chairman is sought the first people to be approached are the merchant banks; for a company secretary — city solicitors; for financial heads — the companies' auditors.

This is not because the old boy network is more rampant in Britain than anywhere else, but simply because interviewing is still a fairly inexact science in terms of guaranteeing that square pegs will be placed in square holes. Even the expert interviewer, when he has developed all his skills, will be left with a strong element of hunch. It is then, and if all other things are more or less equal between the last two candidates, that the opinion of a third party about a man, framed in a way that is relevant to his capacity to do the job in question, can be a clincher. If this is true for the expert, it is even more the case where the interview is being conducted by a manager who has no special knowledge or experience of interviewing techniques and who has either been landed with the job of finding someone to fill a vacancy, dates put forward by the personnel department or consultants. Indeed, in smaller firms, a manager often decides to take a person who comes along with a strong recommendation from a reliable source, rather than go through the rigmarole of advertising, interviewing, and eventually taking a chance on someone who is, after all that, still an unknown quantity. But even if you do not know many people whose word will carry weight with a potential employer, your friends and acquaintances can act as an intelligence service for job leads, as well as helping you to advertise your availability by word of mouth.

But before you jump to the conclusion of the well-known saying 'It isn't what you know, but who you know' (which is anyway a good deal less than a half-truth) let us hasten to add that making the most of your contacts requires just as much thought, planning and skill as any other aspect of your job search. Indiscriminate appeals for help, along the lines of 'let me know if you hear of anything', are shots in the dark: you might strike something out there, but you are far more likely to do so if you can see your target, know where to hit it and what adjustment you have to make to your sights. In other words, you should sit down and analyse exactly *who* can help you, *how* they can help you and *what* sort of information they need to do this effectively.

In the first place you have to be clear about where the limits of your contacts' ability to help you lie in relation to your needs and qualifications. For instance, your closest friend may be the financial director of a major public company, but you know that most of the people he mixes with in a business capacity are financial people. Therefore, if you are a production person, asking him to let you know if something comes up is unlikely to take you much further. You have to think of the help he can practicably give you — it may be a recommendation, or it may be information about a planned expansion in a company he knows of — and brief him in those terms. If you look at the situation in this way you will find that the range of contacts who can help you is wider than you had imagined. They need not be people who can actually give you a job or even influential people whose recommendation will pull weight with an interviewer. Anybody who can give you a job lead that you can work on is worth bearing in mind. So you should draw up for your job file a list of all the relevant contacts you have, noting what sort of work they do, how senior they are and whether they know you in a social or a business capacity. These factors will determine what they are likely to be able to do for you.

Business acquaintances

Most people will want to start among their immediate business acquaintances and for someone in mid-career these will often be personal friends as well. If you have been fortunate enough to have been in a job that involves a lot of contact with your counterparts in other companies you obviously start off with a big advantage over those whose opportunities in this respect have been more limited, or who find it more difficult to make friends. But even if your circle is limited to colleagues in your own company do not hesitate to approach them — remember they may have outside contacts, even if you do not. (At the same time, if you are still employed and 'just looking', you should be very careful to talk only to people you can trust absolutely not to gossip around the office, since this can sometimes provide an excuse for asking you to leave.) Don't forget to add to your list former colleagues, superiors or even subordinates who know your work and who have moved on to other firms — even if your contact with them since then has only been intermittent.

You may wind up with a list of 50 people, or it may be only five. But whatever the number it is not enough to phone and say casually that you are thinking of moving from your present position, or that you have left your company and would be glad if they would let you know if they hear of anything. An approach which is casual (maybe for reasons of pride) will invite an equal lack of urgency in the way they will set about helping you. Apart from that it does not give your contact enough information. You may think he knows all about you — but does he? He knows that you are an intelligent, well-informed sort of person who has held a responsible job, who is good company over a dinner table and who maybe plays a useful game of golf. But what does he know of your performance as an executive? It is that which counts.

Put yourself, for a moment, in the position of your friend or acquaintance. He knows you are looking for a job and that you appear to have been, say, an experienced and successful managing director. So now he calls up a contact of his own, whom he knows to be looking for a chief executive. If that contact is at all alert and competent he will want to know what your qualifications are, what you have achieved, what sort of experience you have had and probably why you left or want to leave your last job. If your acquaintance is unable to answer these questions, his contact will respect him as someone who is trying to do a friend a favour, but the effect of his approach on your own chances is likely to be minimal. If, however, your acquaintance can ring his contact and say that he thinks he might have just the person he is looking for, and is in a position to tell him why, you are going to start off with a big advantage over those applicants who have no evidence to back up the facts in the cv.

So instead of just ringing your acquaintance up take the trouble to go and see him or suggest a meeting over lunch or a drink. You will want to keep things on the informal footing of a business meeting between equals — for that is what it is — but that does not mean to say you should not be getting down to brass tacks. Give him as much specific information as possible — the kind of information you would want about an executive who was being recommended to you; but do not ask him for a job, even if you have reason to believe he might have an opening for you. He knows you are looking for one. You have placed the facts about yourself at his disposal. Let the initiative come from him. You have asked for a meeting, not a job interview, and a request of that kind, if he is unprepared for it, might be embarrassing for both parties. In any case your contact will usually want to discuss the matter with his colleagues before talking to you in more detail.

But even if your acquaintance is unable to come up, then and there, with a concrete suggestion about whom you might approach, the mere fact that you have given him some hard information about yourself, your qualifications and your achievements will enable him to start thinking meaningfully about possible job leads. When he does come up with a suggestion — now or later — that you approach some firm or other which he thinks might be looking for someone of your calibre, don't just note the name of the company; get as much information out of him as you can. Find out about the problems and opportunities presented, what qualifications you have that might be of particular interest to them, what the gossip is about them, whether your contact can suggest

any specific person you should write to, and whether he knows any third party who can give you further information of use in an interview.

Assuming your contacts are just that — not close friends — it is a good idea to send them an informal note of thanks after you have spoken to them. Apart from the fact that such courtesies are always appreciated — even where they are not expected — it serves a useful purpose in giving your acquaintance a record of your address and the telephone number at which you can be reached. You can also, of course, put down any further points which you might have forgotten to bring up when you met.

Having sown the seeds, the awkward questions arise of when and how often you check to see whether they are taking root. Too frequent calls can become an embarrassment to caller and recipient alike; equally, if you make no attempt to follow up your original enquiry, this might be taken as a sign that you have lost interest. The best plan is to make a note in your job file, showing when you spoke to your contact, what suggestions he made and what you did about them. Let about a month elapse before reaching him again and telling him what has happened. From the nature of his response, and his general manner, you should be able to get a good idea of whether it is worth keeping in touch with him, or whether it is best to let the matter drop quietly.

Top-level contacts

Your circle of contacts may embrace some people who are 'big names' — major business leaders, government ministers and suchlike. An endorsement or recommendation from someone at this level can obviously be invaluable, but in general terms it should be appropriate to the calibre of job you are seeking. If you are in middle management a recommendation from a nationally known chairman of a large company may seem somewhat inappropriate in terms of the job you are after, unless you can show that he knows you in a business, rather than a social capacity — as might be the case, for instance, if you are both on the committee of some public or professional body. An endorsement from someone with whom you make up the occasional four at golf is better than nothing, of course, but it is not likely to produce much information about your managerial abilities; and it is obviously a mistake to ask someone for that kind of recommendation if the person concerned is only in a position to talk about your social or athletic gifts.

Unless you happen to know your intended contact quite well, it is generally best to make your initial approach in writing rather than by telephone as your call will first be routed through, and will probably be garbled by, secretaries and personal assistants. Your letter should be brief; don't go into details. Here is an example of the kind of note that, at this stage, should be quite sufficient.

> Dear Sir Leonard,
>
> You may remember that, as export director of John Wilson Ltd, I served with you on the organising committee of the British week in Stuttgart. I have since then decided to leave Wilson's, and I wonder whether I could take up a few minutes of your time to get the benefit of your advice on any opportunities that might be open to a man with my kind of experience in export in general and in the textile business in particular.
>
> May I phone your secretary in a few days to find out a time that will be convenient to you?

Short, to the point, containing a reminder of the circumstances under which you met (important people, like the rest of us, may not immediately connect names with faces or events), positive without being aggressive and implying an understanding that your visit will not take up too much of his time — such a letter should produce a response; and if a date and place is suggested in writing you should, of course, confirm that you will be there.

Handling the meeting

You have promised not to take up more than a few minutes of your distinguished acquaintance's time. This might mean 15 minutes or half an hour. From the atmosphere, the pace of the questions and answers you will probably get the feeling of how long you have to put over your message. There might even be a hint at the beginning that he is pressed for time. But if there is to be any extension of the meeting let it be at his prompting, not because you've failed to think clearly about what you want to put across. Be brief and specific. You are looking for a new job. Tell him so and tell him why. The reasons should be positive: you feel you need a change, more responsibility, a more responsive climate for your ideas — or simply that you feel you are worth more than your present firm is prepared to pay you. Do not — and this cannot be stressed too strongly — run down your present employers or air any grievances that you think you might have. If they are in a mess or having problems the chances are — at least with a big company — that this fact is well known. Your interviewer will respect you all the more if you do not raise the matter.

However, you have come here for a purpose, the same as that with which you have approached your other acquaintances — to outline what qualifications, experience and achievements you have to offer and, in the light of these, to get ideas on openings, or potential openings, for them: names of companies, names of individuals and inside information on special situations in which your talents would be of value to a potential employer. Unless you have been working at the very highest levels yourself, however, your acquaintance is less likely to come up with anything on specific job situations. It is more probable that he will suggest names of people you might get in touch with. Where this is the case it is perfectly reasonable to ask him to give you an introduction by telephone or letter; indeed the most valuable result of your visit might well be that it will open doors that would otherwise be difficult to enter. Leave it at that, though; don't ask him to 'put in a word for you', or anything like that. It is enough, in the first instance, that a very highly placed individual is suggesting to someone he knows that you might be worth talking to. VIPs do not waste each other's time by suggesting they interview a nonentity.

References and recommendations

Just as your request for help should be linked as far as possible to the specific form that help might take, so references and recommendations should be thought of in the context of a specific job situation. It is a good plan to tell your referees as much as you can about the job you have applied for — send them a copy of the advertisement or job specification if you can — and tell them why you are interested in this particular appointment. Writing references or answering discreet telephone calls is an onerous chore so do all you can to ensure each referee is well primed by sending a cv.

Character references should be approached with caution. Open references are virtually worthless but one that can attest your honesty in handling the club's funds or your standing in your local community can set at rest the fear in an employer's mind as to integrity, especially if you are about to be given a much freer hand in your new job.

Choose your referees with a specific job in mind; do not use the same ones over and over again. Some will carry more weight in one type of job, some in another.

Always tell your referees that you have quoted their name for a specific appointment even if they have given permission to use their name in principle — and let them know the outcome with a polite note of thanks for their help, not only as a courtesy but as an indication that they should now cease their efforts on your behalf in this particular situation.

The type of people you should consider among your contacts include:

- former bosses
- former subordinates
- senior executives you know well in almost any company
- clients
- customers
- contacts made at seminars, trade fairs and at official company functions
- the company's auditors, solicitors, brokers and bankers
- personal friends.

A letter asking a friend for a reference might run something like this:

Dear John,

You will remember that you very kindly offered to allow me to use your name as a referee when the occasion should present itself. May I now take you up on this?

I have been shortlisted for a job as head of the division for management development and training services for the Machine Manufacturers' Association, and they have asked me to provide a personal reference.

I am sending you a copy of the advertisement that I originally answered and which sets out the job specification. I imagine the most helpful kind of reference you could give me would be one that would spell out how successful, from your knowledge of my career, you feel I would be in handling the job they have outlined.

Many thanks for your help.

6. Answering Job Advertisements Effectively

You have now begun to put out feelers and have contacted those people who might be in a position to help you directly or indirectly. Now you are moving to phase 2 and about to scan the national press, specialist press and journals in your own field for suitable vacancies. You still have a reasonable amount of time and should use it to the full. This means applying for *every* job in your target area which meets your salary requirements. Do not half-heartedly pick at this task as some people do, resentful of the fact that they are having to look for a job; you cannot afford to let *any* opportunity pass at this stage. Apply yourself purposefully and systematically every day and make sure that every application is your best effort. Don't hesitate to approach employer B while you are on employer A's shortlist. If you end up with two jobs to choose from, so much the better. In most cases it is going to take you quite a time to find the right post and the more you try for, the greater the probability that you will succeed sooner rather than later — provided that you apply for suitable jobs, of course.

Begin by scanning the publications rapidly and mark any advertisements of interest. Then go back and re-read them, cutting out those you decide to follow up. It is essential that you are realistic about this. If you don't meet at least two-thirds of the specification you will be wasting your time and giving yourself needless frustration.

As a broad generalisation job advertisements are now better written — especially those of the consulting firms which specialise in recruitment advertising — but many placed by well-established, specialist agencies still leave much to be desired. To be charitable this is partly the fault of the media owners who do not lay down sufficiently high standards so that the advertiser who insists on his copy being printed, however inadequate it may be, invariably gets away with it. The headline, sub-head and lead-in should show clearly to whom the advertisement is addressed and reflect the USPs (unique selling points) or excitement of the job. Succeeding paragraphs should give sufficient information for the right people to read between the lines and get a feel of the size and measure of the job and its responsibilities; this should be in the context of the company — location, activity, size, turnover or other critical data; an outline of the candidate — by age, qualifications, experience and outlook; the principal terms of contract — salary, main fringe benefits, holidays, and finally the action required. The typical consultant's advertisement will give all of this in under 150 words.

In practice, many employers describe jobs in terms of the qualities they would like to see in candidates with a generous element of wishful thinking. Highly critical factors such as salary, location, principal accountabilities are omitted (they might give too much away!) or so little is said that the whole thing is quite meaningless. So caveat emptor! If the advertisement is specific you have few problems. Either this job is for you or it isn't; either you fit the candidate specification or you don't. In other words, the advertisement does the preliminary sifting for both employer and candidate. Many research studies have been published telling employers what candidates look for in job advertisements but few employers seem to take much notice!

So if advertisements lack critical information — and probably 75 per cent do — you have to learn to interpret them (rather like those of house agents). One could produce a glossary of terms which would include:

'well-established company' — old-fashioned, well-meaning but out of date

'progressive' — just beginning to see the light of day and feeling their way slowly

'dynamic' — hard-driving; probably US-owned and strongly marketing-oriented.

Beware the long list of desired personal qualities — the advertiser hasn't a clue what he wants, and hasn't thought out the job — he just has a hazy idea of the sort of person he wants. As this is likely to be an idealised portrait of himself

25 years ago, you learn quite a lot about the employer! Absence of salary invariably means they don't know how much to pay — and want to get away with as little as they can. (They will know how much *not* to pay — as you will find out!) Or it could be that they lack a coherent salary policy, or have a paternalistic policy, or they fear the unions, or they are just bad payers. 'Salary commensurate with qualifications and experience' (usually inadequately described if at all) almost invariably means a poor salary. A number, however, give broad guidance which is quite acceptable provided that it is not too vague: the salary band — 'candidates earning less than £10,000 are unlikely to have had sufficient responsibility'; 'starting salary will be up to £12,500 but could be more for the exceptional person'; 'salary will be negotiable around £15,000' (ie £14,000-£17,500) — is adequate for you to know whether or not you are in the target area. Often salary is the most important clue to the seniority of the job or how management regard a particular function. You can see two jobs advertised in almost identical terms; for one the salary is over £13,500, for the other £10,000.

The style of the advertisement — wording, lettering, general appearance — will invariably reflect the image of the company as an employer as well as a commercial entity — even if the advertisement has been set by the medium's own type-setters. Flamboyant and racy = marketing-oriented; stilted, full of clichés = formal, rather inward-looking; use of 'in' words like 'accountability', 'objectives' = up-to-date management (but possibly only just so and the consultants haven't yet left). From its wording you can learn the style of management, its attitude towards its staff, its orientation (money, people, production or sales) and from your experience you can fill in the details with a fair degree of accuracy. It is important to weigh every word in the advertisement or you could miss the fact that they need an acceptable professional to bring them up to date or a steady administrator to stabilise the organisation after a period of rapid growth but for commercial reasons dare not say so openly.

In choosing which advertisements to reply to, select the most promising (probably those with salary, location and an outline of duties) and reply to them first. Speed is critical. Don't leave it several days before you reply — 48 hours is the norm. Employers expect to receive the best applicants among the first or second batch and may call these people for interview without waiting for the others to come in. So the longer you leave it the smaller your chances of an interview — even if you are well qualified. So leave to last those in which you are only marginally interested. If you are outside the specification make sure that you give a very good reason for applying. As a rule of thumb five years outside the age bracket either way is acceptable unless the advertiser has been very categorical, ie 'candidates must be under 45'; and about £500 either side of the fixed salary will be considered by even the most rigid employers unless a salary band has been quoted. The advertiser's specifications are guidelines but don't make a fool of yourself and stray too far outside these parameters — it only leads to frustration and a waste of valuable time. Also don't try to read too much into the advertisement. Study it soberly; if there was any really attractive facet it would probably have been mentioned. Study how the employer sees the job and how he describes it and try to interpret this from your own experience and *then* project yourself into the incumbent's chair.

The initial reply

Before dashing off your application re-read each advertisement very carefully — especially the part which says how candidates should apply. The danger is that when you have replied to lots of advertisements you become careless and confused and so fall into serious errors. The initial reply is the most important one of all. If you are in doubt as to what is required play safe and send a brief covering letter with a well-prepared general curriculum vitae (cv). This should be two pages long at most and must set out clearly the principal facts about yourself (see Chapter 8). Keep the covering letter to the point.

> Dear Sir,
>
> I am most interested in your advertisement 'Manager for a new £15M factory' which I read in today's *Daily Telegraph*. As you will see from the cv which I enclose, I have had seven years' experience managing a comparable plant at which the techniques used were probably very similar to those you will employ. Prior to that I had ten years' experience in the design/development and production engineering departments. I am now looking for the opportunity to help build up a new manufacturing unit with a

forward-looking management team.

I could attend for interview at almost any time with about three days' notice.

Your ref DT/35

Yours truly,
John Smith

If the advertiser invites you to write for an application form do just that. Don't bury him in sheaves of references and work samples!

Dear Sir,

Marketing Director — ref ST/125

Will you please send me further information and an application form for the above post advertised in today's *Sunday Telegraph.*

Yours truly,
John Smith

Even if you send a full cv it is highly probable that you will simply be asked to fill in an application form (with apologies, it is hoped) as many personnel people like to have all applications in a standard form to facilitate selection, or they may use a special type of form.

Sometimes, when there is likely to be an exceptionally heavy response, employers make it harder to apply. 'Please state briefly how you meet each of the requirements' or 'in your reply indicate what particular contribution you would be able to make'. These need to be thought out carefully and drafted so leave them till last unless you are especially interested in the appointment advertised. In practice the best bet — and the least time consuming — is the submission of your summary cv and a brief covering letter in which you draw the recipient's attention to the highly relevant experience you have had. Obviously bring out your best points but do be honest and don't claim to have done things you haven't done or put your age back five years — you'll be caught out eventually by the pension scheme and probably lose your job without compensation.

If you don't quite match the exact specification but have very relevant experience draw this out: 'Although I do not have a degree in electrical engineering I have been an associate member of the IEE since 1967 (via HNC and part III) and I have done exactly the same work as the graduate engineers in this design office ever since.' The employer requires knowledge and understanding of principles and the ability to apply them more than paper qualifications and often demands a degree to ensure a certain minimum standard. Of course he may have some other motive (such as acceptability to the rest of the team) but this is unlikely. When the advertiser calls for a letter of application and a cv he usually wants to learn not only your basic qualifications and experience but your ability to present your case clearly, concisely and persuasively — itself an important attribute in an executive. Don't over-sell yourself; personnel people are cautious, and fairly stolid, not given to sudden wild enthusiasms, and most will be irritated by the hard sell.

It is vitally important, therefore, that you spend a lot of time and trouble to get your initial letter just right. Keep a copy of all your letters if you can and as time goes by look back over them and try to evaluate why some worked and some did not. One of the major reasons why people are rejected before interview is because they have submitted a scrappy, ill-prepared initial letter of application which has probably done scant justice to their very real abilities. This may seem unfair but it is a fact — especially if there is a large response, and 150 replies are common. First impressions are more important now than at any other stage; the selection process has started. Here are some tips.

1. Start by stating which job you are applying for, where the advertisement appeared and when. This will ensure that in a large organisation your letter is correctly routed.

2. If your handwriting is very difficult to read have your letter typed. Above all print your name underneath your signature.

3. Include your telephone number in case the company wishes to contact you for interview quickly.

4. Use good-quality paper and envelopes.

5. Lay your letter out attractively using a suitably shaped sheet of paper.

6. If you are sending a cv make sure that it has been neatly typed and laid out. If you cannot do this yourself there are agencies which will do it for a modest sum. Good photocopies are acceptable.

7. Do not fill your letter with heavy crossings-out or obvious corrections. It may be a bore but it will be worth your while doing it again.
8. Keep copies of your letters.
9. Apply only for the job advertised. Do not say that you are prepared to consider other vacancies if your qualifications are not quite up to the mark. If you do you have eliminated yourself already. Should there be another vacancy that might be suitable and of interest to you the interviewer will soon be in touch with you.
10. Do not go into the reasons why you left each job. No doubt you will be asked this at the interview. Be careful how you indicate your present employment situation. The simple fact 'I have been declared redundant' — or 'owing to the closure of company x I am now obliged to look for a post etc' is quite sufficient. Don't go into rambling explanations and preferably don't mention the redundancy unless it is clear from your cv that you have been out of work for some time; it looks like a defensive ploy. In letters of application it is wise to remember what Disraeli said about political leadership — 'Never apologise. Never explain.'

Those forms

When you receive an application blank to complete — in spite of your very comprehensive cv — don't just scribble in the principal details and think that's it. Application blanks seem invariably to be designed by people who have never had to complete them (or they live in nameless houses in cities with two-line addresses or have very little imagination). Space when it is most needed is at a premium (and vice versa); questions are repetitious or obscure, and there is either insufficient room to do justice to yourself or else you are faced with four blank pages to fill. Very off-putting. It is vital, therefore, to study the form in detail before starting to fill it in. If you can, take a photocopy and use that both as a draft and your file copy. Always draft out your replies to the narrative questions to ensure that what you say is relevant and gives as many facts as possible. If space allows it is worth typing your replies for ease of duplication but this requires considerable patience and care. (Many forms are not con-

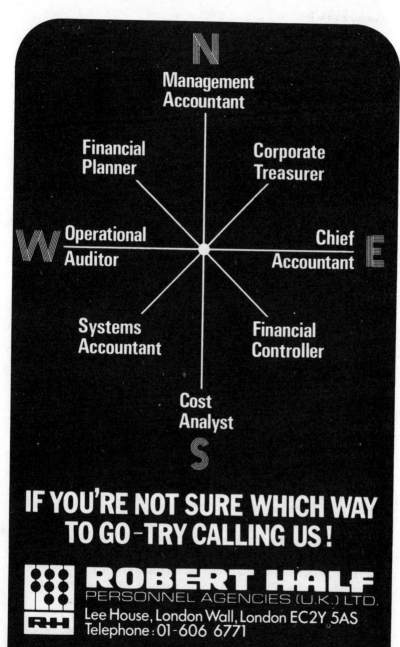

sistent in their lay-out, and lining up the boxes is often a work of art.) Above all, write clearly — most forms are photocopied these days so that each interviewer has one. Do answer *every* question; the form will be returned to you if not and valuable time will have been lost. In practice you need to allow two or three hours to complete an application blank, though there are some which can be done in under half an hour. It is permissible to put additional details (or to continue the answer to a question) on a separate sheet of paper if space really is at a premium — but keep it brief; you run the risk of its being detached.

When returning your completed application blank send a brief covering letter as a matter of courtesy. It is quite a good idea to indicate when you could or could not attend for interview in the next three weeks, but don't make it too complicated or unnecessarily hard to fit in. The addition of the phrase 'I look forward to meeting you (or Mr —) in the near future' leaves a courteous impression.

If you don't get a single interview after all this you are clearly applying for the wrong jobs!

The importance of accuracy

In today's conditions — and as far as one can see into the future — the competition for executive jobs is intense. When faced with a large number of applications, the almost irrestitible temptation for the interviewer is to throw out those that look scruffy, are inconsistent or inaccurate. It may sound schoolmasterish to say so, but do make sure that little things like the dates on your cv are correct and do not overlap. After all, if an applicant cannot write a proper letter or fill out an important form with due care, what is the interviewer going to feel about his ability to carry out a senior job?

The other point that has, unfortunately, to be made concerns honesty. There are some people who, under pressure, are tempted to stretch the truth in the hope that this will improve their prospects — to claim qualifications they have not got, overstate their salary, understate their age, or whatever. In these days of accurate personnel records that kind of deception will always get found out and it can permanently damage your career chances. Hard? Unfair? What would you do on the other side of the table?

Korn/Ferry International
Executive Search Consultants

Korn/Ferry International is a long established and leading world wide firm of Executive Search Consultants. It has been operating in the U.K. since 1967 and currently has a professional staff of 10 in its London Office.

Senior Appointments

Korn/Ferry International specialises in recruiting well qualified men and women from a wide variety of disciplines for appointments carrying salaries in excess of £12,000 per annum. The Company is retained by a wide cross-section of leading British and International Companies and Organisations.

Method of Work

Each assignment involves a considerable amount of intensive library and field investigation. As background research material, extensive and up-to-date files on companies, industries and executives are maintained.

Changing Your Job

The services of the firm are retained by client companies only and the help it can offer to individuals is, of necessity, limited. The assistance however may be significant and senior executives who are thinking of changing their jobs may, if they wish, send us a copy of their Curriculum Vitae. This will be acknowledged and carefully compared with the requirements of current and future assignments, but will not normally lead to a meeting unless there is a close matching of experience and qualifications.

Enquiries

To: David M. Munns, Managing Director,
Korn/Ferry International,
2/4 King Street,
St. James's, London S.W.1.
Telephone: 01-930-5524

Branches in *New York, Los Angeles, Atlanta, Chicago, Cleveland, Dallas, Houston, San Francisco, Stamford, Brussels, Frankfurt, Paris, Caracas, Mexico City, Monterrey, Guadelajara, Rio de Janeiro, Sao Paulo, Hong Kong, Kuala Lumpur, Singapore, Sydney, Tokyo*

7. Consultancies, Agencies and Others Who Can Help You

Apart from friends and personal contacts you can get some free help from most employment organisations — if you go about it the right way. Many will give you a few minutes or up to half an hour of face-to-face advice on your cv, your marketability, salary expectations, the state of the market or general advice. If you are offered ten minutes don't try to take an hour but do make that ten minutes really work for you. Think out in advance what you want to know; have your questions ready; send your cv in advance, and don't argue! You are getting something for nothing and it could be very advantageous to you. Such organisations usually have a market position, that is, they specialise by job function, level or industry. This you can determine from the advertisements they place for themselves or their clients. Any employment agency or recruitment consultancy worth its salt keeps its ears and eyes open for its clients in general and will put forward an outstandingly good candidate who would fit well into a client's organisation, or keep his details on file for the future. To have seen you as well even if only briefly greatly strengthens your candidacy. But they can't see everybody. So choose the organisation with care (good ones will also recommend others), prepare your papers carefully and fit into their systems; you have everything to gain and nothing to lose.

In addition there are dozens of organisations who will give you advice — for a fee. Caveat emptor! Make careful enquiries before parting with your hard-won savings and examine the credentials of the advisers. For advice about a fundamental career change go to a qualified *occupational* (not clinical) psychologist or a well-established firm of psychologists and pay for proper professional advice. It will cost far less than that offered by the more trendy career advisers and be safer. Vocational guidance can cost as little as £50 to £70 and will be scientifically based. If you want advice on how to go about the whole business of getting another job the career counsellors offer both advice and help. This will include help in producing a good cv, advice and coaching if needed in being interviewed, and lots of help in identifying openings in the market, writing letters of application, financial advice (if you are out of work), etc. They will also print cvs for you — but beware: these are easily recognisable and not all create the right impression or are well presented in the eyes of many employers. An employer wants facts, not puff. Some of these organisations are purely advisory and 'help you to help yourself'; others will do all they can for you short of turning up for interview! Buy what you need, and don't be talked into more. This book contains most of the practical advice you need.

Finally, there are firms who offer a limited service such as rewriting your cv and duplicating it or producing your cv in their housestyle and then marketing you through monthly publications or at request. These will want to see you and formally interview you so as to be able to answer questions. In 1981 the cost of these services varies enormously from several hundred to several thousand pounds. Another step well worth considering if you lack formal qualifications or are seriously out of date is a refresher or business course at a polytechnic or business school. In some circumstances these are free; contact the registrar for advice in the first instance.

A multiplicity of organisations are available to help you (see Appendix E) and the following notes may serve as a general guide to the uninitiated.

Executive search

These are usually small firms (most have less than five consultants in the UK) and they deal at the top end of the market. At the time of writing this means salaries in excess of £15,000 pa (UK) and either functional heads, rare specialists and company directors, partners or their equivalents. Some specialise in certain functions or industries. Staff tend to be ex-senior executives, ex-general management consultants and a sprinkling of psychologists. They are usually over 35. Their stock-in-trade is a depth of knowledge of how organisations work and an ability to match people both to the jobs and organisations. They operate very confidentially and are often privy to long-term company plans known only to two or three people in the client organisations. Their advice and help can therefore be very valuable — even if it is no more than a nod or shake of the head at times. Most maintain registers of likely candidates but some are more selective than others. Some are part of an international organisation and have excellent contacts overseas. Most act discreetly and few openly advertise. Fees are charged to companies, not candidates.

Management selection concerns

These companies do a similar job to the executive search concerns, the main difference being that they advertise when they want candidates and tend to deal with both middle and senior management — and to a lesser extent top management. On the whole they are not really interested in speculative applications. Where the executive search firm may introduce a 'good' candidate to a client on spec, the management selection firms are primarily interested in filling jobs which have been notified to them. Some sift candidates largely on paper or on short interviews; others probe deeply. Some are offshoots of employment or advertising agencies; others are offshoots of management consultancies. Staff vary widely in background from experienced ex-line managers or personnel specialists to clerical administrators with an entrepreneurial flair. Their advice will therefore vary widely in its depth and value. Again, fees are obtained from employers, not charged to candidates.

Executive registers

There are one or two consultancy-type operations which operate for employers on a register basis. They advertise in the press regularly to top up their registers but are always glad to hear from 'good' candidates. Fees are charged to employers, not candidates.

Government and official appointments

Official bodies must be seen to be impartial and so recruitment and selection procedures have to be open and non-discriminatory (in the widest sense). All appointments are (said to be) advertised in the national and trade press. Some Government departments advertise discreetly for 'temporary' staff but permanent career appointments are dealt with by the Civil Service Commission at Basingstoke. Some fringe organisations (quasi-government — such as public corporations) sometimes advertise but are known to use executive search methods as well; and Government departments have been known to search for highly confidential appointments, though this is rare.

Executive careers advisory firms

In recent years we have seen the growth of a number of firms whose business is to advise and help senior candidates market themselves. Some have US parents, others are indigenous. Some employ occupational psychologists, some psychiatrists; some full-time executives, others a range of part-timers. Essentially they will advise you on your future career prospects, help you to write letters and prepare applications, school you in presenting yourself effectively at interview, and generally advise. They are not strictly employment agencies. Their business is to advise and help the individual to help himself. Fees vary widely from about £500 to several thousand pounds (15 per cent of previous salary is becoming the norm) — and we suggest that the best is not always the most expensive!

Employment agencies

These cater mostly for junior, professional and lower management grades. Some are general; some functionally specific (accountants, nurses, secretaries, sales personnel, catering staff); some service certain industries (advertising, pharmaceutical, etc). Theirs is a quick-turnover business. Essentially they do a casual, rapid matching of candidate with company. Charges are made to employers rather than candidates though their business is a type of brokerage because they are concerned with both candidate and client company. This is a

CHANGING YOUR JOB?
WE CAN HELP!

As specialist advisers we can help you *plan* your career changes through our systematic and objective approach which has helped thousands of our clients make the *right* career decisions.

With our help you can:

HIGHLIGHT your goals and ambitions to establish what you are really looking for in your career.

IDENTIFY how and where you can be most successful and effective through an analysis of your strengths and weaknesses. This analysis includes tests of aptitudes, interests, values and personality and an in-depth psychological consultation.

ACT to obtain or create the opportunities you need to satisfy your ambitions and make the most effective contribution.

To find out how for less than £100 we can help *you*, phone or write for our free brochure:

CAREER ANALYSTS
Career House
90 Gloucester Place, London W1

01-935 5452 (24 hrs)

cheerful 'short back and sides' High Street service in general, and is especially valuable for those seeking to relocate rapidly in a very small area.

The PER

This is a hybrid Government agency spanning both the employment agency sector and the management selection sector. Being a national organisation with computerised records and terminals, it extends the employment agency concept to cover a nationwide area. It is essentially a vast data-bank of people, the onus being on the individual to select his own job in most instances. However, in addition they advertise appointments either confidentially or openly (ie revealing the employer's name or not as the case may be) and act as any other selection concern. Staff tend to be Civil Servants with a background in industry or commerce.

Professional associations, institutions, university/college appointment services

Much depends on staffing and the way they are constituted, but many of these organisations offer a service of some kind to help their members (or former students) to find alternative employment. Some will carry brief advertisements or announcements in newsletters; others keep lists which they will release to potential employers on request; some will approach specialist consultants or employers; others will give personal advice. Although many of these services are often more of a good-will gesture than a formal service to members, they can be very effective indeed. Charges are not normally made unless advertising is involved, when the charge is usually quite small.

Note
See Appendix E for a list of the main management consultants and advisory agencies.

8. Résumés, Application Blanks and CVs

There are many ways of presenting yourself to a prospective employer, from a telephone enquiry to a fully comprehensive dossier. Let us examine the principal ones you are likely to come across.

The telephone call

There are three types of situation when the initial contact will be by telephone: you may be invited to telephone direct after one of your personal contacts has paved the way; or the advertisement may invite applications by telephone — 'candidates should ring Mr Jones on 123 456 during normal office hours or 789 923 at other times'; or you may be approached by a 'head-hunter' to whom you have sent your cv or who may have heard in a roundabout way that you are on the market. The telephone is used primarily for speed, convenience or discretion. Where an appointment may be difficult to fill or candidates cannot write easily (eg construction engineers out on site) the telephone is considered to be the main means of recruitment.

When you ring it is as well to be prepared for the type of questions you are likely to be asked. Your cv will act as an *aide-mémoire* for names, dates, etc. In addition, try to work out what the interviewer is likely to want to know — the critical factors on which he will decide whether or not to invite you to interview. If necessary, draft out a few concise replies. Here are some typical questions and answers.

Q. *Could you give me a brief picture of yourself?*
A. Yes. I am aged 35 and have a second class Mechanical Sciences Tripos from Cambridge and have spent the last 14 years with two major engineering concerns where I have specialised in the design of steam

turbines for power stations and ships. Most of my experience has been in design and development though I did spend a period of two years seeing a new type of machine through the production workshops. For the last four years I have been Assistant Chief Engineer — Special projects with . . .

Q. *What are your professional qualifications?*

A. I have been a full member of the IMechE since 1969.

Q. *How many people do you supervise directly?*

A. 30 — mostly qualified men, including ten draughtsmen, three technical clerks and five admin staff. When a special project is approaching the production stage the production engineering staff report to me on technical matters.

Q. *I described the job to you very briefly just now. Tell me, what attracts and what you are looking for?*

A. I heard a paper read by your Mr Robinson at an Institution seminar about six months ago and liked the sound of the work you are doing, particularly in the realm of size reduction but with increased output. As you may know, this company has decided to cut back its development work and so your advertisement is of special interest to me.

Q. *How soon could you be available?*

A. Could I suggest the 1st . . .

Q. *Would there be any problems about your having to move to this area?*

A. No. Of course I should have to move house and find new schools for the children, but as they are both under eight this shouldn't be a problem; and my wife isn't working.

Q. *The salary we have in mind is about £11,500: how does this compare with your present salary?*

A. It would mean a bit of a drop; I've been getting £12,000; presumably there would be scope for rises within the salary bracket?

Q. *Oh yes, the scale runs up to just over £14,000 and in any case I think that we might be able to match your present salary. Is there anything else you would like to know at this stage?*

A. No; I think you've covered the critical points and presumably everything will be gone into in detail at the interview. Would you like me to send a cv?

Q. *Yes please, that would be helpful. Let me see, could you be available for interview towards the end of this week — say Thursday?*

A. Yes. The afternoon would suit me better if that's all the same to you.

Q. *Shall we say three o'clock then? I'll drop you a line to confirm it and tell you how to get here.*

The approach 'out of the blue' from a head-hunter is much more difficult to handle as it will take you unawares — even if you have sent your cv to a number of people. When you receive this sort of call you need to be cautious; it is easy to be carried away and to regret it later. The caller will use a semi-informal approach:

Caller. Is that George Fortescue?

GF. It is.

C. Good evening. You won't know me but my name is John Smith and we have a mutual acquaintance in Frederick Johnson of the merchant bankers. I'm a management consultant and have been asked by one of my clients to help fill a very senior appointment. From what I have heard about you I think that you might be a very strong candidate for this post. Could you be interested in making a move?

GF. I see. Well yes, as a matter of fact I could. Are you able to tell me more about the job and your client at this stage?

C. Yes indeed. This is all in the very strictest confidence but my client is . . . etc.

The caller will give you a brief outline of the company, the job to be done and generally try to convey the attitudes of the management as well as the scope for the new man. He will also want to know what the candidate is looking for in terms of career and financial prospects. The call will usually end with the invitation to meet and discuss the appointment in detail.

This type of phone call is difficult to handle as you don't know what is coming and so cannot be prepared. Nevertheless, the work you did earlier when you analysed your needs and your past career will be invaluable in helping you to keep your feet on the ground and enable you to answer those awkward questions, 'What exactly are you looking for?' and 'What is the minimum salary that you are prepared to accept?' It's a good idea to keep the summary chart you made of yourself within reach of the phone so that it is always to hand when required. Of course, if you are not consciously 'on the job market' you will not have gone as far as this but if you are thinking of looking around then this self-analysis, tedious though it may be, can prove to be time very well spent.

If you have contacted the executive search firms and sent them your cv the caller will simply concentrate on the job, the salary, whether or not you are really interested and whether to arrange an interview. Usually, when the searcher has got to the point of giving you a ring he has virtually decided that he would like to see you.

The cv

The next gradation is the cv — curriculum vitae ('the course of one's life') or 'track record' as the Americans call it. It is simply a record in chronological order of the facts of your working life and other relevant details. It should be neatly tabulated and set out on not more than two sheets of paper and it is as well to prepare or order at least 50 copies. If you cannot type it yourself (and no longer have a secretary) agencies will do this for you relatively cheaply. It should cover in order:

☐ *Heading:* Curriculum Vitae
   Your full name

☐ *Personal details*
   Date of birth   Age
   Marital status   Children's ages
   Home address   Telephone number

☐ *Qualifications*
   Your highest academic attainment: whether this be GCE O or A level, HSC or degree, HNC etc
   Subjects and degree class or distinctions
   Professional qualifications
   Any other *relevant* qualifications

☐ *Experience*
   List in chronological order, beginning with the most recent and working back, the dates, names and addresses of companies worked for — set these out in capital letters for rapid scanning — and follow this with a *brief* synopsis of each of the posts you have held, saying what your duties were. Bring out major achievements. Avoid meaningless in-company titles; your correct title may have been 'Chief Personnel and Industrial Relations Officer — Technical and Administrative Staff' — but a more meaningful title would be Staff Manager! Use quantitative data whenever possible — tonnage per month, sales, rate of cash flow, return on capital invested, number of staff, number of work or distribution outlets, profit record, etc. The purpose of this section is to give the reader a feel of the type of work you have done, the environment in which it was done and the size of your job — and hence the range and depth of experience you have had.

☐ *Papers, patents and publications*

Give details such as subject matter, date, name of journal or publisher. Explain the subject matter — briefly — if it was very obscure or specialised. If it led to any practical result — eg if your patent was taken up — that is worth mentioning also.

☐ *Other appointments*

List any appointments of note you have held at work, in a professional organisation or in your private capacity. The latter needs to be handled with discretion, though. Some employers are not enthusiastic about possible clashes of interest which may arise in terms of time if you are active in civic affairs or politics. Equally, outside business activities may be felt to be a distraction from the job you are being paid for. However, if in either case they produce a spin-off that may be useful to a prospective employer, they would probably be regarded as a plus factor.

☐ *Languages*

If you can conduct business in another language it is worth saying so, giving the degree of your fluency.

☐ *Leisure interests*

Be careful how you express your outside interests. Simply list the principal ones by activity and an indication of the depth of your interest or involvement: 'secretary and team player for Bromsgrove Tennis Club'; or 'play golf twice a week — 10 handicap'. If you say too much or list too many things potential employers may (rightly) conclude that you are a nine-to-five man. The difficulty is that employers will interpret this section in an individual and perhaps biased way. So play safe — but don't leave it blank or they will think you're a soulless automaton who simply watches TV every evening.

☐ *Salary*

As a general rule, put current or last salary and a synopsis of principal fringe benefits rather than 'salary required' unless you are prepared to move at the same salary or less. The latter, however, is tantamount to an admission that you are negotiating from a position of weakness, unless you can point to special circumstances, as may indeed be the case with an older executive who no longer has children to support or an ex-serviceman who has a substantial pension. Thus, a good reason for accepting a lateral or downward move in salary should always be given.

Some people prefer to include salary in their covering letter for reasons of confidentiality or flexibility. Nowadays also, because of the instability in some salary structures to which we previously referred, the reason why you are being paid so much (or so little) may need some explanation in your covering letter: 'Company X pay upper quartile salaries as a matter of policy.' Or 'Because of the effects of the recession on Company Y's trading picture, salary rises were held at five per cent over the past two years.' The main thing is that you must mention your salary somewhere — coyness in this respect will work to your disadvantage, particularly since many organisations file cvs within assumed salary brackets.

There is a growing tendency to use a phrase such as 'I shall be looking for a salary package of around £12,000', or 'My salary indicator is in excess of £25,000.' What the candidate is often doing (advised by one of the specialist advisory bodies?) is to put a monetary value on previous total remuneration — that is, salary *plus* all benefits (car, pension etc). This has the effect of apparently grossly inflating — to the uninitiated — the apparent salary demand and there is a risk of misunderstanding to the detriment of the candidate.

Some people still persist in trying to hide their present salary on the pretext that 'the employer should pay me what I am worth'. One has sympathy with this view but if you adopt this approach you should be aware of three factors:

(i) Most employers will automatically assume that you are currently receiving a much lower salary — ie that your present employer doesn't think very highly of you.

(ii) Salary is an indication of the status of a function in an organisation. Job titles and descriptions are often almost indistinguishable but salaries for what are apparently identical jobs can vary widely. This is because salary tends to reflect authority and responsibility levels and not just the ability to perform a series of tasks.

(iii) If you don't give some salary indication — or other means whereby a fairly accurate estimate can be made — you may be rejected as being out of the running.

You will note that no reasons are given for leaving jobs, principally because the decision to move is a complex one. Rarely is there one overriding reason and you will want to stress different factors to different interviewers in different situations. Also, even if there are any skeletons in the cupboard, there is no need to parade them in public! Salary progression is best left out as it can so easily be misinterpreted. So much depends on the interviewer's intimate knowledge of salary scales, the purchasing power of the pound and other factors such as local pay rates, company policy, location and so on. Besides, you may have moved deliberately for less money to a rural area in order to gain first-rate experience.

This cv can be used for almost any job; it is factual and gives the critical information most employers want to know. You will note that nothing has been said to bring out any special experience and no references or names of referees have been given as these are all variables.

The résumé

This will vary considerably with the type and level of job and can be the bare bones of the cv or a long, narrative account of your main achievements written up with a special bias. The sales/marketing person will write a special one for each company selling himself by drawing out all his relevant experience — and suppressing the rest! He will blow his own trumpet and sell himself hard — and this will be expected of him; if he can't sell himself what chance is there that he will be able to sell the company's products? The more senior person will prefer the softer sell and treat it as a letter; others will prefer to use a gimmick (advertising people are especially prone to this) or the form of a report. The older person will give more weight to the last 15 years and only an outline of earlier experience. In other words résumés will vary considerably, are highly selective and depend very much on the job. In essence the candidate is selecting himself for the job by showing how closely he meets the requirements and by bringing out any bonus he can offer. The assessor will also study it for gaps and inconsistencies.

A good résumé should be interesting to read. Everything it

says — or omits to say — is of interest to the employer and so is the way it is presented and expressed. Fortunately, by now, you have all the raw data you need from your detailed self-analysis to tackle this hurdle. Every time you sit down to write one it will be worthwhile referring to the original analysis, partly to keep your feet on the ground, partly so that nothing of importance is forgotten, and partly because it will trigger off other ideas. Probably the best way to tackle a narrative résumé is to put yourself in the interviewer's shoes and ask yourself what you would want to read. To summarise:

1. Make it interesting. Use plenty of paragraphs and keep to one topic at a time. A mere collection of facts is meaningless unless related to the background of the company; a rambling prosy recital is simply not read beyond the first page. Make it easy to take in and make it flow so that it can be scanned quickly.

2. Highlight the important points. Don't clutter it with trivia and irrelevancies or vital facts will be lost in the verbiage.

3. Give it an overall shape so that the reader can go back and pick out points of interest later without having to wade through page after page.

4. It is a good idea to work out a plan beforehand. Reduce each paragraph to one sentence — that is the point you want to make. Then illustrate it with factual references.

5. If you have time draft your résumé in full. In this way you will be able to make it sharper and livelier by taking out anything that is prosy or irrelevant.

6. *Always* read it over for errors (your husband or wife will spot spelling and grammatical errors too).

7. If you have difficulty with your style of writing get a friend to help you with the early ones and then use these as models for the rest.

Many résumés received by employers or placement consultants are meaningless in spite of a lot of time and thought in their composition because they fail to give any reference framework. The fact that the individual has had experience in a range of techniques is virtually meaningless without it. Take, for example, 'I have experience of selling'; unless the employer knows what has been sold, to whom, and the individual's freedom to negotiate, this phase has very little meaning. Similarly, the name of a company — however well known — does not tell the reader which particular products the industrial engineer has worked on, the methods of production employed, etc. 'I raised productivity by 50 per cent' . . . well done! — but what was the baseline you worked from? How did you do it? What was the market trend? 'I raised productivity by 50 per cent by scrapping a trouble-some machine, investing £35,000 in a new Gerhardt moulder and redeploying two ancillary workers' means something to an employer and tells him how you tackled the problem. Finally, avoid the bragging 'puff'; it puts people off and almost always sounds unconvincing. 'I am a first-class organ-iser, motivator and dedicated to my work' is less impressive than 'With a regionalised salesforce of 35 demoralised people in six months we increased sales from £2M to £3M by establishing task forces, introducing tele-link computerised stock requisitioning and a new sales training programme.'

The dossier

If you decide to apply for a job abroad — especially in the USA or Europe — you will need to produce a personal dossier. The international organisations such as the ILO warn British applicants that many otherwise excellent candidates are rejected without interview because they give too little infor-mation. If you are in any doubt as to the form your applica-tion should take contact the appropriate embassy — the commercial counsellor will readily advise you.

To begin with, your dossier needs a good cover that won't show the dirt. Ideally, you should Letraset your name on the front with the words 'Personal Dossier — Confidential'. Choose either a cover with a flap pocket or one with the means of keeping the papers in order and undamaged. The inside should be divided into sections: Personal Details, Education and Training, Work Record, Other Interests, Publications, Testimonials. You will need a good pass-port photograph which should be affixed inside a transparent envelope securely on the inside front cover. Make sure that your name and address is on the back of the photo in case it is separated from the file at any time. Lay out the dossier as you would a special report. Use separate sheets of paper

113

with headings for each section and space things out attractively. Include photocopies of your actual degree or other certificates such as professional memberships and, where possible, written testimonials of your work – you may have to ask for these. Make this a comprehensive affair. 'Personal Details' will include height, weight, health record; information about your family – ages, names of children, your wife's maiden name and nationality; where you were both born; NI number, bank account number – in short any information a future employer might need. The work record should start with a single sheet summary of all the jobs and positions held in chronological order with dates. Then you will need to do a detailed break-down of each job using organisation charts and giving details of accountabilities, actual duties, allocation of time and so on. Of course, you will only need to do one of these as a photocopy could always be made if an employer wishes to retain part of it. Usually you will take this with you to the interview although it might have to be sent by registered post.

Application blanks

The good application blank is a useful selection tool; the bad one a 20th century refined instrument of torture! If you strongly suspect that an application blank will be sent irrespective of what you may have said in your initial letter, send a brief letter of application and enclose a photocopied cv – just in case. Nothing is more soul-destroying than having spent hours on a résumé to receive back an application blank and standard covering letter from a secretary.

Application blanks tend to fall into three categories: personal profiles, general purpose personnel forms, and those devised by psychologists.

1. The personal profile
This is the simplest form of application blank. It was originally designed by one of the authors and is based on the summary a personnel officer will usually make of any letter of application. It was conceived as a combined letter of application and outline cv, and contains just enough information for the personnel officer to decide whether you are a 'possible' or an 'outright reject'. The form has the advantage of speed

(from both points of view) and ensures that the critical information is received first time. It can be completed literally in 15 minutes. The usual procedure is for the advertisement to say 'Candidates should ring 123 456 or write for further information and a personal profile.'

The information you receive has been drawn up to enable you to get a feel of the company as well as the facts of the job. The end result is that those who complete the profile are 'good' candidates. Some employers will interview on the strength of this information; others will invite you to interview but ask you to complete a much more searching document in the meantime. It is worth making sure that you give *all* the information asked for in the profile as only the bare essentials are asked. But don't go into long explanations; just stick to the facts.

2. The general purpose personnel form

There is an enormous variety of forms in this category, ranging from one to eight pages. Some will have been designed especially for this appointment (the Civil Service Commission do this) and so every question is relevant. Some are so general that parts are either irrelevant or too scant. Try not to be put off by this. If this is obviously a form devised for all staff grades from school leavers to senior executives you will have to 'translate' sections to suit a person of your age, even substituting an alternative heading if necessary, eg some forms are not designed for graduates but the employer will really want to know what you did at your last place of full-time education, so substitute 'university' for 'school'. In other places there will not be enough space — as is usual in the 'jobs held' section. The simplest plan is to write it out on a separate sheet of paper following the pattern of the form. Put your name on this sheet and secure it to the form and write 'see separate sheet' in the box on the form. Another hazard with this type of form is that you suddenly find a question difficult to answer — and then discover that it isn't relevant to the post you are applying for! Look out for this if you are a non-technical man applying for a post in a very technical concern; the chief security officer, personnel manager or financial controller is not expected to know the technicalities of scientific processes.

Many companies make the application blank serve as

a personnel record as well. This is confusing to applicants who find some questions suspicious or misleading. Others contain questions concerned with longer-term career planning — but until you know more about the structure and opportunities within the company these are impossible to answer as set. The best plan is to write 'to be discussed' for these.

Another thing to watch out for with this all-purpose form is the lay-out. It will probably have been designed by 'paperwork' experts with very little regard for the person who has to provide the information, with the inevitable result that spacing is appalling and questions repetitious. This is a very real hazard if you complete the form with a typewriter as a sudden change in lay-out may be masked by the machine.

If very personal, private information is asked you are quite within your rights to withhold it at this stage but disclose it in confidence at interview; for example, you may be living with the wife of someone else in the company but don't want every little records clerk to know it. Alternatively, you can write a private note and send it sealed and marked 'personal and private' to the personnel director.

Much frustration is experienced by candidates who receive an endless succession of application blanks and so the tendency is to delay completing them or to fill them in rapidly. Neither course will help your purpose. You simply have to study each form and grit your teeth.

What do you do if the application form does not allow you to do justice to your application? This is difficult — if you ignore the form and send a full résumé you will be regarded as a maverick or as being lazy. The best plan is to complete the form as best you can and either send two to three sheets of additional information or attach a copy of your cv. If you have the facilities it is a good idea to draft your application on a photocopy of the blank form first. And, of course, always draft out the answers to searching questions.

Some forms are used as a selection tool. The personnel consultants and the more sophisticated firms do this. Virtually everything asked will be highly relevant and will fall into one of two sections: (a) historical information, or (b) self-analytic and projective. The latter may be in narrative form or a sort of personality inventory. 'Trace the course of your career and show how well you are prepared to undertake this assignment' is a typical type of question. These narrative questions are the most important ones that are likely to be asked and largely replace a preliminary interview. It is important when answering them to think them out very carefully, viewing them from every possible angle because, while at interview you have the opportunity of making additional explanations and answering supplementary questions, here you have one chance only — and you don't have the benefit of seeing your inquisitor or the company premises beforehand. It may be worth while looking up *Moodies British Companies Index* if you know very little about the company as this will give you some information about staff policy and indications of the background of the directors.

All general purpose personnel forms have to be approached with caution. The early, historical part is easy enough. In the latter part every word written — or subtly avoided — will be studied. As a well-constructed application form can be a more reliable selection tool than an interview, consultants draw up a long shortlist of about eight people from their study of the forms. The questions asked will probably have been researched so draft your answers with care. This does not mean that they are looking for straight conformists; far from it. What it does mean is that, as your voice and facial expression are absent, your words must speak for themselves. Try reading what you have written in a toneless voice to see if it affects the meaning in any way. A standard answer will not do either, as your answer must reflect the job you are applying for. Incidentally, if at a later date you apply for another job through the same consultants, ask to see and, if necessary, revise your application blank as it may well contain sentiments or reflect a bias which would be totally wrong for this new appointment.

3. The psychologist's blank
This is one other type of application blank which you may have to fill in. Some companies refer all shortlisted applicants for senior positions to specialist appraisal firms who will compare you with successful managers on an international scale. Or it could be that you wish to change your whole career and have decided to see a vocational guidance psychologist. You can easily identify this type of form as it is usually 'weighted'

117

and 'scored' as you can see from the figures in the margins. It will also be more searching in its form of questioning. Much more detail will be required on such things as your academic performance by asking for the actual marks or grades you achieved in all subjects taken, and you may find it necessary to look up the original certificate. If you cannot find it the Examining Board will tell you (perhaps for a small fee) if you give them details of when and where you sat the exam. This type of form often contains a personality questionnaire and some very tricky self-portrait and self-analytical quest-ions. Or you may be asked to complete a questionnaire or to draft a board report on a given topic or similar business exercise.

The psychologist is trying to determine what makes you tick. He tries to build up a picture of you in action and within the environment of your life. He plumbs the depth and range of your knowledge and experience, the use you have made of the opportunities you have had, your behavioural pattern, your motivation, career aims and so on. And he is looking for signs of maladjustment and strain. It is difficult to complete this type of form honestly and dangerous to try to 'cheat' your way through it. The only thing to do is to answer it as fully as you can and try not to present yourself as a paragon of virtue or to let your imagination run riot. There is a strong temptation to try to be too clever in answering this type of form, which must be resisted at all costs — or else you will reveal too much to your disadvantage!

A psychologist's blank may take you three hours to com-plete and will seem a frightful waste of time. On the other hand it enables you to give 'perfect', well-thought-out answers away from the stress of the face-to-face encounter, and with your stocktaking analysis you have most of the raw material you need anyway.

There is a growing tendency to use slightly off-beat selec-tion techniques. One of these is graphology. Unless you have anything to hide (!) it is worth ensuring that there is at least one sentence somewhere in your own fair hand, otherwise there will be yet another exchange of letters and delay.

Here is a checklist to run through before you complete yet another application blank.

1. Re-read the advertisement and any other information you have received or have ascertained.

2. Make a list of the critical factors in the specification.
3. Take a photocopy of the form if you can.
4. Study the form for its content and lay-out.
5. Draft your answers to the tricky questions.
6. Check these against the list of critical factors. Have you done full justice to yourself? If not, redraft.
7. Complete the form carefully in black ink, black biro or type it (for ease of photocopying).
8. Check your answers for legibility, spelling and grammar.
9. Is there anything important you have omitted because it has not been asked? If so prepare some additional notes, refer to these on the form and attach them together firmly.
10. Check that you have signed and dated it and have your name on the additional notes.
11. Despatch it with a brief covering letter without delay (the recipient will look for dates and postmarks).
12. Have you put the job reference number on the envelope? If not, do so if it is going to a large firm or to a consultant.

9. How to Make an Impact in the Interview

All your efforts to date in analysing the job market and in launching yourself on it with the help of skilfully prepared résumés and with leads and recommendations from agencies and friends have had one end in view; and in the first instance it is not, you may be surprised to learn, to get a job but to get an interview. That is a hurdle you will have to overcome whether you walk straight into a company chairman's office with a warm recommendation from a cabinet minister, or whether, after a long and worrying wait, you have managed to get to see one of that same company's personnel officers about a post as, say, one of a team of estimating engineers on a new project. It is vitally important, therefore, that you are equipped to handle every stage of every kind of interview at every level. Never make the mistake of thinking of it as a formality, or of an initial appointment with a man at a lower level as a tiresome preliminary to the hard stuff on the short-list. You are on trial every time and each situation must be one that you negotiate cleanly and successfully.

More noticeably, perhaps, than elsewhere in the book we talk in this chapter of the people concerned – in this case interviewer and candidate – as being male; purely in the interests of syntactical simplicity. The principles of interviewing and being interviewed are the same for women as for men, so the male pronoun used in this context should be read in a unisex sense.

Planning the preliminaries

Opposing generals in wartime try to find out as much as possible about the commander they are facing: his background, his education and how he fought his other battles. The man who will be on the other side of the desk to you is not your opponent, but there is an analogy here. The more you know about him and his company, the more you will be able to anticipate his questions, plan for them and answer them tellingly.

If you have gone to your library and consulted the references we set out in Appendix D (useful sources of information) you will have found out quite a lot about the company already: exactly what it does, where it operates, how many branches or subsidiaries it has, how it is expanding geographically and in terms of activities and processes, what it specialises in, how it sells its products, where it stands in relation to the competition, what progress it has made in recent years and what its problems are. If its products are on view anywhere, go and look at them and try to find out discreetly what customers and retailers think of them in terms of quality, price, delivery dates and any other information that may be relevant to the kind of job you are looking for. If there is any company literature around, try to get hold of it. Maybe the firm has a showroom. An hour there might be well spent. Another good idea is to get hold of trade journals in which the company features and to keep a close eye on the business sections of the press before the interview. It is not only a question of finding out specifically about the firm's activities. At a senior level you may be asked questions about the general economic climate and intelligent opinions and background on this can be gleaned from papers such as the *Financial Times* and *The Economist*.

As mentioned previously, do your best to learn something, if possible, about the man who will interview you: this will be easy if the meeting is through an introduction from one of your important contacts. Before it takes place, get as much information as you can about what sort of people and attitudes he likes and dislikes, what aspects of the business he takes most interest in (obviously you should check up on those), what his general background is, what his personal interests are and idiosyncrasies you might have to watch out for.

Unfortunately personal information like that is often hard to get, but even if you have no close acquaintances in common it may be possible to find out a good deal. If the man you are going to see is operating at the top level, you may be

able to look him up in *Who's Who*; some professional bodies
and institutes also publish directories of members which give
at least a minimal amount of information about them.
Another useful source is *British Qualifications*, which will tell
you exactly what the initials after his name mean; this may
also give you some clue about his background and special
interests. If you already know somebody in the same company it will be worth while having a word with him. Even
if he personally doesn't have anything to do with the man
you are seeing, almost invariably he will know someone
who does. Most people are glad to help in this way. Another
useful piece of preparation to undertake will be if the job
involves travel abroad or contact with foreign customers. If
you have given a language as one of your qualifications, make
sure you are ready for one of the interviewers to spring a
question in that language on you. Before the interview,
therefore, you should refresh your knowledge of business
vocabulary by reading and, ideally, by practising conversation. The international editions of *Reader's Digest* and
current affairs weeklies are invaluable sources of current
business terminology. A good substitute for the latter, if
you have access to a tape recorder, is to use it to talk to
yourself, so polishing your fluency and checking your accent.

Making your entrance

The letter you have received calling you for the interview
will specify a time and, if the place is not easy to find, will
probably tell you how to get there. Don't be late, under any
circumstances. Most people hate to be kept waiting and are
apt to regard it as both discourteous and a sign of feckless-
ness in the latecomer. You should give yourself plenty of
time for the journey, therefore, and an allowance for the sort
of thing that can go wrong — traffic jams, for instance.
Remember also that if a map of the area was sent with their
letter it may not be quite so clear on the ground as it looked
on paper. Getting there half an hour early will give you time
for a brisk, tension-relieving walk. Being ten minutes late will
almost certainly mean that the odds are stacked against you
before you have said a word.

Sometimes, of course, the boot will be on the other foot
— you are the one who is kept waiting. But even if the time is

drawing out beyond what you consider reasonable it is important to keep your cool. If this happens a polite enquiry to a secretary is in order, but any sign of impatience or irritation should be avoided. These may be observed by subordinates and their opinions, both favourable and otherwise, have a habit of trickling back to superiors and may influence the impression they get of you.

Mostly, though, the interview will take place more or less on time, and any spare moments you have between arrival and being called in can be very usefully filled in by checking over your cv and any other papers you may have brought with you or by thinking up some further questions that may arise during the interview and how you would answer them. If you are in an anteroom, trade literature, catalogues or house magazines may be laid on the table. Studying them may provide some piece of background information that may come in very useful during the interview; it may also help to relieve any tension that you may be feeling.

You and the interview

Your interviewer may be a man in the personnel management hierarchy who has been made responsible for recruitment. In other cases he may be the person you are going to work for or the divisional head to whom he is responsible. In some senior jobs you will probably meet, at some stage, a panel of interviewers who will include members of the top management. Yet another alternative — the most common one at the pre-selection stage for senior appointments — is that a firm of consultants will be handling the interview for a client to whom they will pass on the candidates whom they consider most suitable.

Like other kinds of company executives, interviewers come in all shapes, sizes and abilities. Some are experienced and competent, know what they are looking for and know what sort of questions will enable them to establish whether you fill the bill. Others will leave it to you to make out a case for yourself — which is much more difficult than developing it in response to questions. If you are being interviewed by someone you will be working for directly, it will often be that, having satisfied himself about your qualifications and that you know what you are talking about, he will probably con-

centrate on the specific dimensions of the job and how you fit them. In other cases, the interviewer will be more interested in getting some kind of picture of your experience, interests and personality. Some interviewers will be polite, others — perhaps intentionally — will be awkward. There is no stereotype for interviews, any more than there is for other kinds of human encounter. The important thing to remember is that an interview is just that. It is not an ordeal, it is not a humiliation and it is not your last chance; it is a business meeting in which you think you have something to sell and the interviewer thinks you have something to offer — otherwise he would not have asked you along.

The consultant's interview

The typical consultant's interview will take 1½ hours and follow a rather different pattern from the face-to-face meeting with a future employer. The consultant is an 'honest broker' and has to weigh the needs of both candidate and employer. His interview is therefore a two-way affair. Starting with a description of the client company and job he will give his interpretation of the scope of the appointment from the candidate's point of view. This may well take the first 20 minutes of the interview and will include some discussion and the invitation to ask questions. When it appears certain that the candidate is genuinely interested in the appointment the consultant will begin the interview, usually by leading a discussion based on the needs of the company and how the candidate might set about solving them. Questions of fact will be interspersed from time to time. The discussion will then move to the career and personal needs of the candidate and to what extent this appointment will meet them.

Essentially this type of interview is a matching process and involves overt self-selection by the candidate as well as the gathering of evidence on which the consultant will eventually make his judgement. Typically the interview is a more informal and more friendly affair (but no less searching for that) than the interview with an employer — except at very senior levels when a similar approach will be adopted. After all, if the candidate is a good one the consultant will want to consider him for other jobs if this one is not entirely suitable. The difficulty with this type of interview is its permissive-

125

ness. It is very easy to be caught off your guard and the consultant, being a trained and experienced interviewer, is unlikely to let any weakness pass unexposed. It is also very flexible and you will be able to choose, at times, the direction that it will take, so be prepared for this. The giving of advice is a normal part of this interview so be prepared to discuss salary requirements and to seek guidance on your asking price — consultants will be very realistic about this and will often suggest that the job is revised to suit your abilities and will 'sell' you to the employer.

Handling the interview

Just as a business meeting has its course — the opening pleasantries, the sparring, the detailed negotiation and then, if it can be reached, the conclusion — so has an interview. But before dealing in detail with the kind of points that will be involved at the nitty-gritty stage there are a number of ground rules which it is useful to bear in mind.

1. Try to introduce your strong points in a subtle, unostentatious way, letting them flow out of the course of the meeting, rather than loosing them off as your opening barrage. Even if you are an executive with uncommon qualifications which have enabled you to achieve a unique record be careful how you talk about them, otherwise you may be written off as a 'bighead'. The facts will be in your cv. Let that speak for itself until the appropriate occasion arises — as it will. Knowing when to say things is just as important as knowing what to say.

2. We have noted earlier that the 'passive' interviewer who lets you make all the running is particularly difficult to handle. It is easy to ramble on inconsequentially and indeed some interviewers adopt this stance deliberately, inviting you to talk about yourself and seeing how you handle the situation. What you should do in that case is to narrow the conversation down to something tangible. This is where your previous study of the company and its activities comes in useful. You should begin by referring to aspects of its operations which resemble work you have handled successfully

and describe concisely and with specific facts what you did in a parallel situation.

Some men find it very difficult to interview and will give you far too much rein for comfort. If the interviewer asks 'Where would you like to begin?' you can ask, for example, if he would prefer that you start with your background in such and such an area, or your experience in dealing with a particular type of situation. On the other hand, some interviewers will deliberately let you choose the subject as a technique to test how well you are able to sell and to match yourself to the requirements of the job.

Don't make the mistake of asking 'Well, where shall I start?' You have been given the opportunity to fight on ground of your own choice. Seize it by conducting that part of the interview through an emphasis on what you can do and what you have done; but remember it must always be related to what you can do for the company you want to join. Don't let your achievements sound like a business obituary. Relate the past to the future.

3. Guard against introducing too much material — irrelevant autobiographical data or details about past jobs that have no particular bearing on this one. For one thing many interviewers rightly regard a man's ability to distinguish important from less important facts as a pointer to his executive ability; for another you may only have a limited amount of time to put over your message, particularly in the earlier stages of selection when candidates are usually being seen at intervals of half an hour or so. Don't get into the position of having insufficient time to dwell on the things that will create the greatest impression.

4. Be persuasive rather than argumentative. Above all, be very careful about being drawn into an argument on matters of fact unless the point you are making is a vital one. Your interviewer may have his figures wrong on the annual tonnage of cement used in road building, but he will not relish your telling him so. You don't have to back down ignominiously, of course. Say

127

something like 'Well, that point can be easily checked. Let's leave it open.'

5. Don't be offensive, even if you think the interviewer is. Be firm but do not lose your temper.

6. Don't name drop to make an impression — you will probably make the wrong one! However, there are times when who you know is of critical importance in, for example, the consultancy world or in sales. You will sometimes be asked who you know as a measure of the level at which you are used to dealing — but beware, it may be checked out. So keep your name dropping to a minimum unless it is vital to the job.

7. Never, never run down or make snide remarks about your present or any of your previous employers, even if you think you have good cause to do so. If you are in a job but looking for a change this does not necessarily imply criticism. Say you are very happy with the firm, but that you feel the way they want your job to develop does not fit with the way you would like your career to develop — this will give you an opening to put forward some of your ideas to the interviewer. Even if you have left as a result of a blazing row there is no need to go into details unless asked to do so. If that happens explain dispassionately, briefly and unemotionally what the row was about, what your point of view was and how you differed from your colleagues. If you have become redundant as a result of a merger, or rationalisation in the wake of a fall-off in business, say no more than that; though you should be prepared for a question of why your particular post was one of those singled out for redundancy.

8. If the circumstances and specifications of the job you are applying for are explained to you don't, unless invited to do so, tell the interviewer how the job should be done or express any critical opinions about how it is being done at present.

9. Don't apologise for your age. It is a common fault with the over-40 job-hunter to harp on this theme in one way or another instead of stressing his qualifications to

do the job; qualifications which are enhanced and tempered by maturity, not the reverse.

First impressions

First impressions are usually important and you should try to establish a relaxed and pleasant atmosphere with your interviewer or panel of interviewers. If names are mentioned try to memorise them and use them in your answers. You will also find it useful to establish what the position in the company is of the person or persons you are seeing because, as we mentioned earlier, the kind of answers they will be looking for to get a picture of you will depend on the working relationship they expect to have with the person appointed. A man you will be working for directly will be mainly concerned with your knowledge of the ins and outs of the job. A personnel man may be more concerned with a general set of characteristics that fill the job specification he has been given, and longer-term prospects with the company.

Usually the opening stages of the interview will be concerned with clarifying or expanding points in your cv. You should now be prepared to explain the precise nature of your responsibilities in the various jobs you have held, to whom you reported, how your achievements were measured and to what extent you succeeded in meeting the objectives which had been set to you. An alert interviewer will also spot and ask about any unusual features of your career; for instance if you have ever held a job for only a short space of time, or if you made a move involving a drop (or an unusual rise) in salary. Your answers should be truthful, but if there were any points in your past where you came unstuck on a job there is no need to go into lengthy explanations or apologies about it. In any situation of this kind there are always two versions — yours and the other man's — and if you feel your side of the story is the right one, go ahead and give it. You could say, for instance, 'I didn't feel, after a while, that I was quite getting the chance to develop my ideas at ABC Ltd that I'd hoped for, so when I got an offer from XYZ I decided to take it.' Having said that, of course, you should be prepared to answer questions on what exactly some of those ideas were.

The problem question

Having satisfied himself on the basic facts of your career, the interviewer can now get on to establishing how well you are likely to be able to do the job he is hoping to fill. One good way to do this is to put to you a number of problems that either actually cropped up in the job or that are analogous to it. He may take up a point in your cv and say:

1. 'Our Australian agents have a contract with us that has another two years to run, but we're not very happy about their performance. How would you handle that one?'

2. 'I see that at XYZ you achieved 15 per cent increase in productivity by improving labour relations. What sort of problems did you have to cope with? How did you solve them? What did you do first?'

3. 'We have just produced such and such a product. Here it is. We're rather disappointed with the way it's going. Have you any ideas on why it's doing badly? What would you do about it?'

4. 'Let's take the following situation: a manufacturer of lawn mowers is getting complaints from his customers that it's taking too long to get spares. The wholesalers say that it's uneconomic to keep a full range of spares and that it's the manufacturer's fault for taking too long to deliver. How would you solve the problem?'

5. 'Owing to expansion we're thinking of moving our factory away from here. What sort of location would you move it to, and what would be your reasons for making that choice?'

6. 'In the instance above what are the main steps that have to be undertaken, and what would be your priorities in tackling them?'

7. 'One of our plants has a very much higher labour turnover than our average. How would you set about looking into the reasons for this?'

8. 'We're finding it very difficult to get skilled labour for such and such an operation. What can we do about it?'

9. 'You've got some very interesting ideas, but they would obviously cost money to implement. Have you any idea what the scale of expenditure would be? And over what period could we expect to recover our investment?'

10. 'If we were to offer you the job, how would you set
    about seeing what sort of things have to be done right
    away?'

The possibilities for this sort of question are obviously endless and it would be impossible to prepare in specific terms
for their content. However, these instances do illustrate in a
general way the principles underlying them. What the interviewer wants to establish is your judgement, your ability
to express yourself and be decisive and constructive in solving
problems. A mature and experienced executive need have no
apprehension about this stage of the interview. He will have
come up against precisely such situations in the course of his
career, and dealt with them. Indeed in this very fact there is a
pitfall to be avoided. A tendency to talk too much is a
common failing as men approach middle age. Typically such
men have seen and done a lot and therefore have a lot more
to talk about. This can be very interesting at the right time
and place, but not now. What you have to do is to get to the
point fast and stick to it. Avoid reminiscences, and if you
have to relate some anecdote from a previous job keep it
short and keep it relevant. Use your experience, but do not
spell it out in detail.

Will your face fit?

Having assessed your ability to handle the techniques of the
post, the interviewer will then move to some more general
aspects. In particular he will be interested in establishing
how you will be likely to fit in as a person. Consequently he
will ask personal questions and you have to realise that this is
part of his job, even if he is a personnel man who may be
junior to you in years and a good deal down the ladder in
terms of your previous jobs. It is his business to build up a
picture of your stability, your health, your ability to get on
with superiors and subordinates, your interests outside the
job, what sort of books, newspapers and periodicals you read,
your attitude to people of other backgrounds and nationali-
ties; maybe even the sort of friends you have. He will have an
eye both on whether you are likely to get along with your colleagues, and on the fact that as an executive you will probably
be in the position of meeting people outside the firm as its
representative. A firm's representatives, you will appreciate,

are not just its salesmen; every senior member of the company creates to the outside world an image of what that company is and stands for. As far as your personality in relation to the job is concerned, he may also ask you what you feel your strongest (and maybe weakest) traits as an executive are and what aspects of the job you feel you will like doing best. You should think carefully, before the interview, how you will handle a question of this nature. It is almost as important as another awkward one that often comes up with the mature executive applying for a job slightly lower down the ladder from his previous one and can be phrased something like this: 'Aren't you "over-qualified" or "too experienced" for this job?'

Even if this question is not voiced you may sense that it is being implied in the interviewer's attitude to you. In these cases you should find an appropriate opportunity to stress that an executive with your experience needs much less time in which to get to grips with the job. It is a common complaint of employers that a new man is not really earning his keep for the first six months because it takes that long to pick up the threads of what is involved. Like everyone else, you will need time to get acclimatised, but in your case it will take *less* time. As for being over-qualified, you might tactfully point out that in a job and a company which is growing all the time it is an advantage to have a man who has more qualifications than are needed, just as the same company, planning a factory or a warehouse, would build for its needs *ahead* of its present level of business.

Negotiating the salary

Obviously salary is another question you should be prepared to deal with; particularly as it can be said to have two dimensions — the actual salary level you expect and the point in the interview at which the issue is raised.

Where you have replied to an advertisement, usually the salary is stated, either in precise terms or as falling in a certain range. In other instances the salary profile may be more vague: 'not less than £ . . .' or 'a suitable applicant will be unlikely to be earning less than £ . . .' or 'salary will be negotiable in the region of £ . . .'. In all those cases the salary level will be a matter for discussion at the interview; and, of course, it will be of prime importance where you have been asked to attend an interview in reply to an on-spec letter or some other initiative from you.

The greatest difficulty is when the question of salary comes up early in the interview, before you have had time to get an idea of the scope and responsibilities of the position and the opportunity for advancement. Until those details have been clarified any proposals you might make would be based on little more than your desire for a certain sum of money. You should, of course, have decided prior to the interview what your salary aims are and what is the least you will work for — the considerations to take into account are outlined in Chapter 4. But until you know a good deal about what the job involves you are not in possession of the facts that will enable you to negotiate the right kind of figure. Thus, if you are invited to discuss salary matters early on in the interview it may be advisable to suggest diplomatically that more details about the position and your qualifications to fill it should be gone into first, so that you can get a better idea of what you can do for the company.

The interviewer will seldom have a hard and fast figure in mind — but usually he will have decided, or had outlined to him, the maximum the company is willing to pay for the particular job that is being offered. However, if he can get a good man at a bargain price he is unlikely to let the opportunity slip. To that extent, and within certain limits, how good a deal you get is up to you. So what is the best way to handle the situation?

Generally, it will be left to you to initiate the salary question. You should phrase your question by talking about a *starting* figure, thereby implying that you expect your performance to be worth more to the company when you have worked your way into the job. Another approach is to ask what salary range the company has in mind. The use of the word 'range' implies that, although you do not insist on starting at the top if there is room for the job to grow, you do expect your remuneration to increase once you have shown your ability to produce results. Indeed, in general it is a good idea to centre the discussion on future prospects. You might say, once the job has been outlined to you, 'That sounds like a position that will be worth £10,000 in two or three years' time. That could be a very exciting opportunity, so I'll be happy to leave it to you to determine the starting figure.' Such an approach labels you as a £10,000-a-year man who can be obtained for a lower figure now. It also enables you to name a figure which is close to your actual expectations but which, mentioned as a starting salary, might frighten the interviewer off. Even if he thinks you are worth it, it might, for instance, be too much out of line with what he is paying people for similar jobs at present.

This same tactic is a useful one in the tricky situation where you are applying for a job which actually carries a lower remuneration than the one you have been earning. Managers tend to be suspicious of a man who is ready to take a drop in salary and in that situation you might say, 'Well that sounds like something that would put me on about my present level in a couple of years' time. Obviously, I appreciate it'll be a case of working myself into a new job, so there'll be an initial cut involved, but it sounds such an exciting job that I'm willing to take a chance on that.'

Tact is essential at this stage of the discussion. It is unwise to attempt to bargain. You may know your worth; but for the company that is considering you, you are an unknown quantity. The time to raise your sights is when this is no longer the case. On the other hand it is disastrous to imply, as you may be tempted to do if the job-hunting process is not going well, that you might be willing to take the job at less than the advertised salary 'until you have proved your value' or some such phrase. This will not get you the job and it may undermine your morale.

The questions you should ask

As the interview draws to the final stages, you will probably be asked whether you have any questions — whether all the points you might want to know about have been covered.

It is wise and tactful to begin by asking about matters which show your interest in the work — what you can do for the company rather than what the company might do for you. Thus you might start by asking if there is any way you could prepare yourself for the job if it was offered to you; for instance if there is any company literature or job manuals which are available for you to look through. You might also ascertain if there have been any special problems or difficulties which are likely to crop up in the job and which you could think over ways and means of tackling. Apart from anything else this might give you a pointer as to why the previous incumbent of the job no longer has it. The attitude of the interviewer towards your predecessor could be a significant factor when you come to make a decision as to whether or not you can work with him.

If you are going to have staff working under you, this stage of the interview is a good opportunity to get to know about them — what their age and experience is, and in what ways they are most likely to need and respond to your leadership.

Another point worth touching on is whether the company provides any facilities for further executive training in the way of internal or external management courses. For instance, you might say, 'If this job develops in the way you've outlined it, I imagine it will be necessary for me to get some further grounding in financial management. What sort of opportunities will there be, apart from private study, to get more into the subject?'

Of course, this does not mean to say that important matters regarding personal benefits should be left open. While it is not advisable for an executive to ask about hours, you do need to find out how much evening and weekend time you will be expected to devote to company affairs.

Other points that you will want to check are:

1. Whether there is a service contract and what its provisions are. For instance, there might be a clause preventing you from undertaking any outside paid work. If you are, say, receiving an income from writing articles for a professional journal it is important to make a decision whether to give up this work, clear it with your future employer, or not take the job.
2. Whether there is a company pension scheme, when you become eligible for it, and whether it is contributory or non-contributory.
3. Whether, in addition to the stated salary, there are any commissions, bonuses or profit-sharing schemes.
4. If the job involves travelling or entertaining, whether expenses are payable as incurred, or on a fixed allowance; and if the latter, how much it is.

135

5. Is a company car provided, and if so under what terms?
6. If the job involves moving abroad or to another part of the country, is any assistance given with removal expenses?
7. When would it be convenient for the company to have you start work?
8. Will it be possible (in the case of small firms) to acquire a share of the equity?

When you have satisfied yourself on these points — and you should be careful to keep to essentials and not to drag out your part of the questioning process for too long — indicate that you have finished. Don't just lapse into silence, but say something like 'Thank you. I don't think I have any more questions at this stage.'

Some basic interview etiquette

If you have not been used to interviews and are more accustomed to the casual relationship of executive equals it is useful to bear in mind some of the rules of the more formal relationship that governs an interview. The following are some elementary but important points of etiquette.

1. Don't sit down immediately you enter the room. If the interviewer does not ask you to be seated let a moment elapse before you do so.
2. Don't walk into the room smoking and do not light up unless invited to do so.
3. Even if you are nervous, try not to betray the fact by irritating mannerisms such as rubbing your hands, fiddling with a pen and so forth.
4. Look at the interviewer unless he is interrupted by a subordinate or a telephone call. In that case it is polite to glance away.

After the interview

At the end of the interview you may have been given a hint about whether or not you are likely to be offered the job. Perhaps you will have sensed yourself that things have gone your way and that you are in with a chance — or not. Or you may be told that you will have to meet yet another executive before a final decision is made (it is common practice at senior levels to meet the chairman and the Board — usually on an informal basis). If so, do make sure that anything you slipped up on at interview will be well covered next time and if you have any areas of doubt note them down and either check them out or make sure that you find out the answer when you next meet.

But however well the interview went, don't assume that the job is 'in the bag' until you have a firm offer in writing. No news is not necessarily good news because firms may take weeks to make up their minds before turning you down 'with regret'. So don't stop your job search until things are safely tied up; hard experience shows that the chances are 4:1 against you, even if you do reach the shortlist stage.

So now you have done everything you possibly can to get this particular job and you are waiting anxiously for the mail. Perhaps you will have had several irons in the fire simultaneously and, since when one's luck changes it is apt to do so dramatically, you may suddenly find yourself in the position of having more than one job offer. If this is the case you will have to weigh up the longer-term prospects, the considerations of job satisfaction, the reputation of your potential employers as a business and in their attitude towards their staff, the working surroundings, whether you are likely to find your colleagues congenial, and the comparative salaries and benefits of each job. There are a lot of factors to think about and it is right that you should make your decision carefully. But if you are in this position, and want a few days to think matters over, you should inform the parties concerned — don't lapse into a puzzling silence.

Don't leave such a decision open for more than a week at the outside and, having made up your mind, inform the firm you are turning down that you have decided to accept another offer. Once again, this is not only good manners, but good sense. Having spotted you as a promising executive they might at some future point approach you about something even better.

Preparing for the interview: a checklist

1. Have you informed yourself, as far as possible, about the company who is interviewing you or on whose behalf the interview is being conducted? Check the following points:
   (a) its main activities;
   (b) major subsidiaries in the UK or overseas;
   (c) its future plans;
   (d) any problems that it is known to have.

   Sources are company reports, available from banks and accountants in the case of leading firms, reports in the financial pages or specialist journals.

2. Have you polished up any specialist skills or qualifications, such as languages, which you may be tested about — informally — at the interview?

3. Are you prepared to elaborate verbally on your cv?

4. Are you prepared to explain any mismatch between your own qualifications or personal details (such as age) and the job specification in the advertisement? Have you, in fact, taken the precaution of re-reading the advertisement?

5. Are you ready to explain anything that looks like a rough patch in your career?
6. Have you come across questions in previous interviews that you found difficult to cope with? Are you now better prepared to answer them?
7. Do you have a clear idea of what salary to ask for if no figure is specified or only a salary range is indicated? Can you justify it, if your target figure is significantly higher or lower than your current remuneration?
8. Have you got a list of fringe benefits (pension scheme, car, help with removal costs, etc) that you want to try to negotiate?
9. Are you clear about when you can start work?
10. Are you sure exactly where the interview is being held? Have you allowed yourself enough time to get there?

10. Other Methods You Might Encounter

Because it is recognised that interviews are an imperfect selection tool, some employers adopt other methods or reply on the advice of an outside 'expert' — hence the rise of the management selection consultant. What other methods of selection are you likely to have to face? There are five main ones and one occasional one:

psychological tests.
depth interviews
group interviews
behavioural exercises
selection boards
meet the wife.

Psychological tests

There are three main types:

general aptitude
special aptitude
personality.

As you could be faced by all three we will describe all of them briefly.

General aptitude
General aptitude tests set out to measure the extent to which you can solve new problems, your mental flexibility in seeking and finding solutions to problems. For some jobs this is important, especially if there will be a lot of entirely new material to learn. For the older applicant, untimed power tests are usually used. You are unlikely to finish one of these

as they become progressively more and more difficult. Your vocabulary and your ability to perceive abstruse sequences are the principal measures used.

Special aptitude

These measure your reasoning ability with a certain type of material — words, mechanisms, figures, letter/number sequences. They are correlated with a special type of skill such as those employed in abstract reasoning, editing, engineering, accountancy, computer skills and so on. In some cases they assume some previous knowledge and the tester will attempt to assess this separately. Special aptitude tests are mostly used when the individual will have to use a latent skill or develop one in a new job. You are more likely to meet one if you want to change your type of job radically than if you want to continue in your old line.

Personality

There are two types of personality test — projective and behavioural. The projective type, of which the Rorschach Ink Blot test is the best known, asks you to describe the feelings or emotions that are aroused in you by an abstract shape. Responses tend to follow set patterns and the extent to which the candidate's reactions follow one pattern or another is scored. As with all personality tests there is no right or wrong answer; the tester is concerned with the emotional make-up of the candidate and from this is able, by reference to research studies and to his knowledge of human behaviour, to predict future behaviour.

The behavioural tests — 16 PF and the MMPI are the most used — ask the candidate to say how he tends to behave in a number of typical situations. In every case he is forced to choose which action he is most likely to take. Now anyone can deliberately give the answers he thinks the tester wants — but the tester is quite up to this one and will automatically examine the result for an 'ideal' or a 'true' response. After all, no sensible tester will use one measuring instrument in isolation, and it is the overall fit of all the evidence that he is concerned with. A faked test score tells him something about the candidate — but it may not be to the candidate's advantage! The tester enters all scores onto a profile and will usually weigh them statistically to compare them with the

141

norm (if he has occupational norms) or with a population — such as industrial managers. As this type of test gives a behavioural pattern, ie it shows how the candidate tends to behave (or would like the tester to believe he would behave) in certain types of situation, it is relatively easy for him to predict future behaviour in a new job (because people behave more predictably than they think they do).

Some large groups of companies have developed batteries of tests which they have correlated with future progress and 'fit', and they may insist that you sit these before even attending an interview. This is especially true if your qualifications are weak in some area or if the job will make significant new demands on you, for example, working for extended periods in the Middle East or Africa. The testing procedure will probably last a day. Try not to be put off by this. You are in with a chance, merely by token of the fact that the employer is having to pay several hundreds of pounds to have these tests conducted — he is obviously not going to spend that sort of money unless he considers you a possibility. The batteries to which you will be subjected will generally include some specially devised for the company or job but will usually follow the pattern of pencil-and-paper tests with multiple-choice questions or short essays. It is important to take these seriously no matter how senior the job — the company will even if you don't! Incidentally, the tester will often be prepared or offer to reveal the results to you at a later session. This is well worth your while and can give you both reassurance and a deeper insight into how others see you.

Another type of test that is very popular on the continent is the use of graphology. Usually you will not be aware of this unless you are asked for a sample of your handwriting, or you may notice that you are asked to complete a form in your own hand. These tests are particularly favoured in the Netherlands, France and Germany. The results are certainly interesting and generally correlate significantly with other test and interview evidence in the author's experience — though they are often couched in medieval language referring to such things as 'spleen', instead of the more usual jargon of modern psychologists! Oh, and if you are asked for the exact time, date and place of birth, the company may be employing an astrologist (we're serious!).

As legislation attempts to ensure equality of opportunity, so reliance on negative criteria such as age, sex or social background is giving way to more scientific or defensibly objective methods of selection. Trades union pressure may also be significant and lead employers into more elaborate and, for the candidate, more drawn out and tedious selection procedures. However much you dislike them it is as well to remember that they are done for your benefit!

Depth interviews

If you are referred to a consultant for a second opinion he will give you a 'depth interview'. By this we mean an interview lasting around 1½ hours in which you will be asked to think pretty deeply about your work, your life, your motives, goals, philosophy of management, etc. The consultant will be interested in your total existence and in the use you have made of the opportunities you have had in life. Some of this will seem at the time to be of little relevance and many will ask you to recall things you have not thought about for years. Some interviewers will attempt to 'stress' you (they shouldn't as this makes the interview even less valid!) and by putting pressure on you hope to force you to show your true self. This is tedious but if you start to pin him back by asking him stressful questions (eg 'How do you justify the existence of a department of this size when the company's profit record is so poor?' — and if you've done your homework you will probably have more facts and figures at your finger tips than he has) it usually lowers the temperature very rapidly! If you have followed faithfully all the steps in Chapter 3 you will not only take it in your stride but also do yourself full justice.

Depth interviewing is sometimes done by someone trained to observe and interpret 'body language', that is, every movement you make, the way you enter the room, shake hands, sit, movements of hands, eyes, the position of your hands and head when talking about different topics; all of these will be carefully recorded. It is easy to say 'be your usual self' but not so easy to do. The best advice is to be natural and try to relax; sit still, listen, concentrate, look the interviewer in the eye and keep your hands lightly folded in your lap. Try to appear quietly confident and weigh all your answers carefully. And remember, you will be under observation all the time you are in sight! Once again the interviewer may be prepared to give you some feedback at the end — but don't relax your guard; you are still being assessed!

Group interviews or meet the board

Provided that you are well prepared for them, group interviews can be quite fun! If not, they can be confusing and rather terrifying. The usual practice is for each member of the panel to discuss one topic in turn while the others listen, assess and take notes. Five or six pairs of eyes fastened upon your every movement and facial twitch is unnerving at first — unless you are an exhibitionist, in which case it is nice to be the centre of attention. The thing to do is to notice their reactions and facial expressions, assess them, and then play up to them! This is not as difficult as it might sound. They are not on their guard as you are. You will soon find their favourite topic and you can feed them with tit-bits from time to time. This may sound facetious but it really can be done because as a selection technique, board interviews are cumbersome and do not allow that depth of rapport which is the characteristic of a good one-to-one interview. The same is equally true when you have the chance to meet the board. Unless you are very sure of yourself and wish to make a rapid make-or-break appeal it will pay you to box carefully and play safe until you have had the chance to assess the general climate and the balance of power. You should then make sure that the most influential member of the board (you will probably be asked to sit next to or opposite him at lunch) has a good chance of assessing you fairly and that his questions are answered properly — at the expense of others if need be (you will soon learn whom you can politely ignore). It is always dangerous to cross swords on these occasions; far better to compromise and seek out your adversary later if you decide to join them. For this is very much a two-way exercise to see how well you would fit in with each of them and become a full member of the team. From that point of view it is most useful and you should take full advantage of the opportunity given you. You will also be able to assess them as your future colleagues and friends and get a clearer idea of the unique contribution you will be able to make and what experience you will be able to gain as part of this team.

145

Behavioural exercises

All the shortlisted candidates are seated around a table and are given a group exercise to tackle. The assessors are seated around the periphery or take a minor part in the proceedings. They are interested in observing how each individual sets about influencing the others and the role he tends to take and how well he is accepted by the others. In some cases roles are assigned; in others they have to be agreed or fought for! Often two exercises are set: the first, a short, sociological exercise, will be based on the discussion of a controversial topic which may have little direct relevance to the appointment or to the company. The other will be task-oriented. Roles will probably be assigned and switched at intervals. Usually you will all be members of a working party with a highly relevant, well-related task to perform — such as devising or giving your considered opinion upon a policy matter. You will be fed the data you need or ask for.

This method of selection was very much in vogue during the 50s and early 60s but is not so widely used today. It has the advantage that you are all seen in action and in interaction; but it is a difficult exercise to assess, is brutal and tends to favour certain types of people and to show others in an unfavourable light. All these situations are perforce contrived and the whole thing can fall horribly flat. However, forewarned is forearmed, so be prepared!

Selection boards

Basically, this is a combination of tests, interviews and activities designed to provide a wide range of information about you, your personality and your abilities. It is used by many of the larger companies as well as by the Armed Services and the Civil Service. Sometimes it is the precursor to a final 'depth' interview and then must be regarded as a winnowing process before the final decision is made.

Naturally, the procedure varies considerably, but it is a very thorough method of assessment. Candidates are under observation for a far longer time than is possible by most other means of selection and they can be put through a larger variety of tests. To say that there is a foolproof way to succeed would be ridiculous, but there is a definite advantage in having some idea of what to expect. There are also a few sensible preparations you can make to ensure that you show yourself to your best advantage.

The selection board normally takes two days and there can be anything up to eight candidates on any board. It is normally stressed that it is not a competition and that it is theoretically possible for everybody in the group to pass or fail. As part of the point of the board is in seeing a man in contrast to others, it is inevitable that a competitive element creeps in. There is no real harm in this if it helps you to keep yourself mentally sharp.

There are usually three main activities on a board: written tests, verbal group activity and interviews.

1. Written tests

One of the earliest of these is a personal assessment, which can be tricky if it takes you by surprise. You are presented with a blank sheet on which is written a question like 'Write a description of yourself as seen by a friend.' Either together with this, or, in some cases when you have finished it, you get another sheet which says 'Describe yourself as seen by a critic.' There is nothing sinister about either of these questions, but as you will have only a limited time in which to answer, it helps a great deal to give some thought to them before and at leisure. What you are prepared to say about yourself is your own affair, but it is as well not to be too extravagant. Above all, keep the two answers balanced; otherwise you may end up with an extremely hostile friend and an unusually tolerant critic. Try writing a specimen paragraph for each of these; then check it against what previous work reports may have said about you. An understanding wife or a frank friend can be a great help to see that the accounts are neither too idealistic nor too humble.

Other tests are usually of the more conventional intelligence test type. These usually measure verbal, numerical and visual/spatial ability. It is not possible to do very much about one's IQ, but you will find that with a little practice you can improve your score at these sorts of tests. Try several equal tests one after another, and in between, have a thorough post-mortem on your mistakes. You should find that, once you get into the swing of it, your performance will be improved considerably on your first 'cold' effort. (You

147

can obtain books containing these tests quite easily in paper-back form, one good source being *Test your Own IQ* by H J Eysenck, published by Penguin.)

Quite often there are general knowledge questions, usually with a heavy current affairs bias. These tend to concentrate on the names of people in the international news scene, so time spent browsing through an international *Who's Who* should pay off. Certainly you should read one of the serious newspapers thoroughly for some time before the board.

Your final written work will be in the form of a major project or problem. You are presented with a bulky file of assorted information about a particular problem, which may or may not be connected with the body holding the selection board. This usually devolves around the siting of a major factory or installation at several alternative sites, each with its own advantages and drawbacks. There is really no prior preparation you can do for this. There is usually no one answer which is the correct one. You are being tested on your ability to assess and solve a difficult problem. Write down the possible courses of action and the factors affecting each one; then make your choice and say clearly why you prefer it to the other courses available to you. But remember that you are often working against time. and allow yourself sufficient time to write down your answer, whatever it is. At a later stage you may also be asked to draft a letter or a reply dealing with a specific problem, to test your ability to express yourself clearly and, in some problems, tactfully.

2. Verbal group activity

This is the main area in which you will be compared in action with the other candidates on the board. You may be asked to discuss, without a chairman, a matter of current interest, and later to discuss other matters with each of the group taking it in turn to lead. These latter discussions are often connected with facets of the main written problem. You will be assessed from three aspects. What qualities do you exhibit in an un-chaired discussion; are you dominant or passive, but above all, are you constructive? Second, when working in committee under a chairman, can you contribute as part of a directed team? Finally, if you are in charge, can you communicate the problem clearly to your group and are you able to get the best out of the group's combined abilities?

3. Interviews

At a selection board there are usually at least three members or assessors. They will be headed by a chairman, who is usually part of the personnel function of the body holding the board. One of the other members is usually trained in psychology and will be concentrating mainly on your motivation and background. The other one is usually a senior serving member of the branch, department or service which is doing the recruiting. He will primarily be concerned with your suitability for a job rather than the more general approach of the others. You will normally have an interview with each one of the assessors. Sometimes you may have to provide a list of topics you are willing to discuss in some depth. Here, you should avoid subjects which are too narrowly specialised, but they should be things you can talk about sensibly and with a definite viewpoint. This again is an area where a little sensible preparation can improve your performance.

In general you should, unless you are an introvert, enjoy the selection board. A sense of comradeship does develop among candidates. It is worth listening to the comments the others make about an interviewer you have yet to see. If you do not perform well at one test, remember that results are considered on all the tests and that some are more important than others. Finally, though a selection board is by no means a perfect method of selecting an individual for a job, it is certainly one of the most thorough, and does give you a chance, especially if you are changing your field, to be selected for what you are, rather than for what you may or may not have done in the past.

Meet the wife

This is popular in the USA and is used in Britain where a man's wife will be actively involved in his work or where the effect on the man's family will be considerable — such as prolonged absence from home, a job abroad, social work where a man's home will be used, or a board appointment where the man will need to have an accomplished hostess for a wife. People in Britain do not care much for this idea but if one thinks about it, in some appointments, a person's spouse may be a great asset or a major liability.

149

How then are wives assessed? Two popular methods are used and both of them are only semi-formal. The most usual is a dinner engagement where the candidate's wife is invited to be the hostess. The chairman may, in effect, invite himself to dinner (he will probably provide the champagne). He will expect no more than a normal, fairly informal, friendly dinner party and this gives your wife a chance to ask questions as well.

The other method is to invite wives to come to discuss any problems they foresee and generally to ask questions. The major overseas companies provide this service partly to save time (a trained secretary who has been to the country can often answer the questions better than a busy executive and with less strain) and partly out of self-interest; a dissatisfied wife is often the major cause of high staff turnover in overseas assignments — and of course the obverse is equally true.

So your wife need have nothing to fear. In many cases she will have a very enjoyable night out — and it will be you who will be on tenterhooks hoping that you have briefed her sufficiently in case she gets the names or companies mixed up.

11. How to Wait Sensibly - and Maybe Profitably

Studying the press, attending interviews, writing letters, drafting cvs and filling in application forms — all the paraphernalia of looking for a job — is a time-consuming business, and there are indeed those who advocate that it should be a full-time occupation. Whether or not a man is happy to devote all his energies to it is a matter of temperament; and whether he can afford to do so may ultimately boil down to a matter of finance. But many executives whose working life has been a major interest find the lack of a positive activity while they are waiting for the right job to come up a major problem in itself. The danger that also has to be watched, particularly over a longer period, is simply that of getting out of the habit of working. It is important to keep as mentally active and up to date as you were when you were employed, and there are many ways to do this. In some cases, furthermore, they may present the opportunity to bring some extra money rolling in.

Most readers of this book will have thought about the possibility of paid part-time work and will be familiar with the numerous advertisements offering lucrative-sounding opportunities in this sphere. Some of these are perfectly above-board, though they generally involve selling extremely hard a product that is intrinsically hard to sell — no names, no pack drill. Very often, too, the suggestion is that you should try to sell to your friends. Selling to friends something they do not much want to buy is a good way of spoiling relationships and, as we have suggested in an earlier chapter, your personal contacts are much too useful to you in the job-hunting process to be used in this peripheral way.

One must also say that some of these part-time opportunities should be approached with great caution. In any situation where people are forced to look around for a source of income and have some capital available, as is the case with many redundant executives, there are sharks ready to come out of the rocks. If, therefore, any proposal that is being put to you involves your putting some of your own money behind it, it is absolutely vital that you investigate the total situation as fully as possible.

Consult your bank manager, accountant and solicitor (cautious individuals though they may be). They are able to render invaluable service if only in terms of formulating your doubts or asking you to face up to and answer those nagging questions that your enthusiasm has pushed to the back of your mind. The opinion of well-informed City friends will be worth having — even if they have no direct information themselves they may know merchant bankers or business journalists who can provide it. You yourself should also check them from some of the sources set out in Appendix D. Broadly speaking, however, it would not be going too far to say that you should not commit money to somebody else's venture unless you know the people concerned personally or receive a favourable report on them from more than one person whose judgement and integrity you have cause to trust.

Not all the opportunities for keeping yourself constructively occupied are in business; nor do they all produce a direct financial reward. But no doubt most people will think first of all of the ways to augment their income, so let us begin by looking at the area of short-term and part-time employment. First of all, some general principles.

Whatever you decide to go for, your aim should still be to remain very much in the hunt for a permanent job. So, if you are taking an assignment in your own field, and you are aiming to return to it, you would be unwise to take on anything which is too far below the level at which you have been used to working. Apart from the fact that it is bad for morale, it might not look good if it came out in an interview. The next point is that if what you are being offered is something that involves regular working hours and it is going to run for more than a couple of weeks, you should make it clear that you are going to need a reasonable and clear-cut arrangement of time off for interviews: something like one day out in ten, when needed and without payment, might be the sort of basis you could discuss. A third factor to bear in mind is that you should not make a commitment that binds you morally or legally to an extended period of notice.

Very few temporary jobs for executives are ever advertised, but this fact in itself gives a clue to the direction your search should take. The point is that the availability of such work is sporadic and unpredictable: someone falls ill in the middle of a specialist assignment; a report suddenly needs writing in a hurry; an unexpected contract creates a temporary personnel problem; a salesman in a key territory is laid up after a car accident. Circumstances such as these can all create a situation where someone offering his or her services as a stand-in would be welcomed with open arms. But if such a job were advertised, by the time a suitable person was found the need for him would have gone. Therefore, and though there are a few agencies for temporary executive assignments, getting a job of this kind depends very much on your initiative and on being in the right place at the right time.

In an *ad hoc* situation like this, it is obviously difficult to lay down any hard and fast strategy to adopt. Rather, we would like to suggest some general avenues of approach.

1. Put the word around

When you are talking to friends and contacts about a permanent job, mention also that you are available for short-term assignments. Certain skills, of course, are more in demand than others. For instance, business has a considerable appetite for the analysis of financial and marketing information and a smaller firm may not want to go to the expense of bringing in a fully-fledged consultant for this purpose. In such cases an accountant or a numerate marketing person might well fill the bill. Personnel and training problems are also an area where management might look to the help of a skilled outsider who can prepare a report to form a basis for company action or tackle a specific problem such as selecting candidates for supervisory or junior executive jobs.

2. Advertise your availability

Line advertisements in trade and specialist journals are not expensive. Analyse your skills and consider which of them would be of most interest to a firm looking for temporary executive help. Very likely this would not be in an area involving general decision-making, which requires an inside knowledge of the firm concerned, but in tackling short-term, specialist problems. A sales executive from the printing industry, for instance, might phrase his advertisement like this:

> Thinking of selling print to industry? I can prepare a comprehensive report on new opportunities, problems and make specific suggestions on how and where to get business — based on ten years' experience in the field and a wide range of contacts with purchasing decision-taking executives. Ring . . . for further details.

As is the case with your main job search, the emphasis must be on specific assets you have to offer, and should embody suggestions on how they can be used by the person you are trying to reach. Approaches like 'Redundant sales director, early forties, extensive contacts. Any offers?' — and one sees plenty of variations of this theme around — are simply a waste of money.

3. Use your overseas contacts

Your overseas business friends will not be able to help you in the same direct way as those you have at home, but it is worth suggesting to them that you may be available for a short-term assignment in case anybody they know in your field is interested in getting a detailed survey of opportunities in this country. A foreign businessman contemplating an exploratory visit over here could save himself a great deal of time if he comes primed with such information as where to locate his factory, what the labour market is like in a particular area and generally what sort of decisions he is likely to have to take. Once again, you should not only say that you are available, but should also make specific suggestions about the kind of service that you could undertake.

4. Check the agencies

Many of the larger employment agencies, and particularly those that supply specialist personnel, have temporary assignments on their books. You will find them in the yellow pages, often with a description of their activities and specialisations. The PER do not, however, have temporary posts on offer, though Jobcentres do.

5. *Communicate your expertise*

Communication is a growth industry. In a world of rapid change there is a tremendous appetite for information about new technologies and techniques, new economic and social developments and new methods of doing old tasks more efficiently. On the other hand there is a shortage of people who have the gift, the background and the time to communicate this knowledge effectively. If you have specialist qualifications and up-to-date experience you should, therefore, consider lecturing possibilities. Get in touch with consultancy firms offering lectures and seminars in your area of expertise. Professional institutes are often glad to add a good lecturer to their list if they run regular courses. They are also frequently approached about lecturers by outside bodies. Another approach worth making in this context is to the staff training centres of large firms and to the principals of any colleges of further education in your area.

A further sector of the information market where the demand exceeds the supply is in writing. We are not here talking about novels or books for the general reader — where the rewards, except for a tiny minority, are exceedingly meagre — but of technical books and articles. There are about 300 specialist, professional and technical magazines in Britain, the main ones being listed in *British Rate and Data* or *Writers' and Artists' Yearbook*. The editors of these are nearly always glad to be able to use an outside contributor who both knows his subject and can write good, readable prose. Rates vary greatly but average around £40-£50 per thousand words.

Book publishers are always glad to hear from prospective authors in such fields as management, technology, science and accountancy. The best approach here is to write to an appropriate publisher sending an outline of the subject matter you propose to cover, a specimen chapter, a note of what sort of audience the book is aimed at, any competing titles that you know to exist (and why your book is going to be better and different!) and any other relevant details, such as your qualifications as an author. If you have no idea which publisher handles which types of books ask your local librarian or look around the shelves of any large bookshop. Publishers normally pay authors a royalty on the published price of the book — for a first work in hardback this will usually be ten per cent. If he is obviously very keen to do the book you may also be able to persuade him to give you an advance against royalties when you sign the contract.

Keeping yourself up to date

Whether or not your book is accepted for publication eventually, the mere effort of writing it will have two useful spin-offs: it will keep you busy and it will keep you up to date with your subject. Both are important whatever you may be doing. You should keep in touch with all the developments that are going on in your industry even when you are not employed in it. Make a regular trip to a good reference library to read the journals and other important new publications.

Another good way to keep in touch — and to fill gaps in your knowledge — is to attend courses. This will cost you money but it could be a good investment, not only for when you get a job, but in terms of talking more knowledgeably in interviews. The Institute of Directors, through their education department, run a series of short, intensive key courses for directors and executives which are good value although they are not cheap; write to Education Department, Institute of Directors, 116/119 Pall Mall, London SW1Y 5YS. Many management colleges and other professional bodies also run specialist or refresher courses.

Recent years have seen a major change in Government financial help for those whose knowledge or skill is out of date or whose skills have become redundant in our economy. The TSA (Training Services Agency) both run and sponsor students to other courses covering a very wide range of skills. To be eligible you must:

— be over 19 (over 27 for post-graduate courses) and have been away from full-time education for at least two years;

— be at present unemployed or willing to give up your present job to take up training and intend to work in the job in which you train;

— have not had a Government training course during the past three years. This period may be reduced if you are upgrading skills learnt on a previous TOPS (The Training Opportunities Scheme) course;

157

— be suited to the course of your choice (your aptitude and previous experience will be taken into account).

Additional facilities are available for disabled people and certain ex-regular servicemen. All courses are open equally to men and women.

A scale of allowances is paid depending on your circumstances and whether you have to be away from home or not. NI contributions are credited (including earnings-related supplements if eligible) and certain expenses are paid — such as travelling expenses. While these benefits will not equate to a previous salary they are not ungenerous and will cover the basic needs of you and your family. The rates are revised from time to time and are set out in leaflet TSD L 91, available from your local Jobcentre. Courses vary considerably from two weeks for a career development conference to 52 weeks for a Diploma in Management Studies. There are courses at all levels from craft and office skills to senior management and they are run throughout the country. There are also management training TOPS courses for people

intending to become self-employed.

To apply, contact the local TSA office or PER office or Jobcentre and make an appointment to see the Training Adviser. If possible, do your homework first and bring details of the course you wish to attend, together with an outline letter of eligibility by the college concerned — and don't forget details of fees and other costs. There is a book called *Train for a Better Job* available free from the above offices describing the schemes available in detail.

12. New Horizons

When you have completed your self-analysis you may have come to the conclusion that you should try to build your career in another area or apply your expertise in a different way or in another country. Or you might be coming round to that point of view after searching unsuccessfully for a job in your present field; alternatively, you may have a hankering for setting up a business of your own. Whatever the reason, it is well worth considering such possibilities, because for the right person and given the right frame of mind, there are plenty of opportunities around.

The business of building a new career is a vast topic and would need another book to itself if we were to cover it all adequately, though parts of it are dealt with in two other Daily Telegraph/Kogan Page publications: *Working for Yourself* and *Working Abroad*. In the meantime, let us look at the main possibilities.

Self-employment

In recent years successive governments have begun to look with a much more kindly eye on the self-employed, partly because they have been recognised as a highly motivated and therefore highly productive sector of the workforce and partly because an increase in self-employment is seen to be an answer to the unemployment that has become a feature in most industrialised countries. Thus quite a number of tax concessions have been made to the self-employed in recent budgets, of which perhaps the most significant for anyone starting in business has been the provision that losses incurred in the first four years of self-employment can be set off against income, including that from a salaried job, of the preceding three years (though this only applies to sole traders and partners, not to limited companies — a distinction we shall explain below).

To talk about losses might sound a gloomy note with which to lead off, but good accountants have been known to present a convincing case to the inspector of taxes for a business making a loss whose owners are not actually living in penury. This does not mean to say that the possibilities for tax avoidance by self-employed people are infinite, but they are certainly greater than for salaried employees; a case in point being the scope for employing one's wife in the business, where she can earn up to £1375 free of tax. For this and other reasons, consulting an accountant is an essential preliminary to setting up in business and the same is true so far as the services of a solicitor are concerned. There may, for instance, be planning applications which have to be made and which he can advise you about — quite apart from such fundamental decisions as whether to form a limited company or to operate as a partnership or as a sole trader. In most cases he will suggest the first of these options, because if things go utterly wrong for you, your liability is limited to the issued shares and assets of the company, which may only amount to a few hundred pounds' worth. In the case of a sole trader or partnership your entire personal assets are up for grabs by your creditors, should you come unstuck.

The knowledge that your liability is limited will, of course, make your bank manager look at any application for a business loan or overdraft facilities with a distinctly beady eye; and despite talk of government money and venture capital from private sources, for the average small business, the bank remains the principal source of finance. Other funding sources are not really interested in you until you are much bigger and more established (though this may change with the introduction in the 1981 Budget of an important provision granting private investors tax relief of up to £10,000 pa on investments in certain kinds of new companies). The bank will certainly ask you to secure their money in some way more substantial than taking shares in your company and they will also want to keep a close eye on your activities. This is not necessarily a bad thing. A good bank manager will from the start ask you some very pointed questions about the viability of your venture which, if you have not asked them of yourself, you certainly should do because it could save you a lot of grief and disillusionment later on.

The trouble with our increasingly specialised world is that very few jobs nowadays allow one to get the sort of all-round view of things that running a business entails. People at the production end of things tend to have very little insight into how goods and services are marketed. Equally, salesmen and women may have rather inadequate experience of the complexities of production and costing; and neither group may know enough about basic financial procedures, the neglect of which is the most frequent cause of business failure. In other words, a bright idea or a burning desire to get into business on your own is no more than a good start. When you are buying a business you ought to know exactly why the previous owner is selling it and hence whether the price is a realistic one. If you intend to manufacture something or offer a service like starting a restaurant you have to ask yourself who the market is, how you are going to get at them, what they are prepared to pay and whether your product is going to be better and cheaper than the competition's at a price that will enable you to make a living. And even if you have no competitors at the moment it is well worth considering what impact it will have if you get them, because if you are seen to be successful, sooner or later others will copy you. So how are you going to stay ahead? This is a great problem if your success attracts some of the bigger business fish in your waters, because the effect on cost of large-scale manufacture is drastic, as the weavers found out as long ago as the Industrial Revolution. You may get lucky and be bought out at a handsome profit but on the whole it is best to stay away from activities in which big companies are heavily involved unless you have unique skills or knowledge, as may be the case in electronics, for instance.

In other words, how cooperative your bank manager is going to be about money depends not only on your ideas and your qualifications, but on how well you have thought out their application to the venture in hand. He is also going to be very interested in how much financial nous you display. This does not mean that he will examine you on your ability to read a balance sheet, but he will expect you to have prepared, with your accountant, a simple cash flow forecast,

163

showing expected income and outgoings over something like a three-year period. Again, this is an excellent discipline from your own point of view as well, because apart from forcing you to think hard about all your costs — and hence what you should be charging — it will also highlight such matters, easily overlooked by the beginner, as the need to keep a tight rein on debtors.

There are, of course, some questions to which only you know the answers, but they are as important as any of the others. These relate to your aptitude, in general terms, for running your own business and here you have to look objectively at your previous working life. Are you good at making tough decisions about people and at taking financial risks? Have you been successful as a manager? What aspects of business are you good at or less good at, and which of each are liable to be brought into play here? Above all, are you prepared to devote most of your waking hours, for the first months and possibly years, to your work? Self-employment is an exacting path down which to tread, and as with mountaineering, character and stamina are as important as the right equipment.

Franchising

Taking up a franchise is a method of setting up in business on your own which has attracted a good deal of attention in recent years and is growing rapidly — the number of retail outlets alone has doubled since 1978. Essentially a franchise is a form of licence which, on payment of quite a substantial start-up fee, entitles a company or an individual investor to use the name and methods of a parent organisation in making available a product or service. The licence will include: (a) an obligation on the parent to provide continuing assistance in such areas as publicity and management guidance in return for payment, which may be a share of the profits, a royalty on gross turnover, a premium, or a mark-up on the supply of goods; (b) a provision for the introduction of some capital by the investor; (c) area protection — not invariably given — and possibly options on additional areas. Further, the parent company may make a number of other services available to the investor — special training, the advantages of bulk purchasing and, in cases where the construction of premises is involved, help in site selection and the obtaining of permissions, the drawing up of plans and the supervision of building work.

The attraction of franchising is that it gives the investor the good will attached to an established name and the blueprint for an operation that is already proving successful elsewhere; but although there are a number of reputable and well-run parent companies in the franchising world, there are also some that do not fall into either of these categories. Therefore, proceed with caution; and before you do anything else, consider whether a franchise of the type you are contemplating taking up makes commercial sense in the location being suggested. Insist on being given a list of several people already operating the same type of franchise and question all of them. Franchise salesmen can urge haste, but avoid paying deposits and make no commitment until you have completed your enquiries.

Be quite sure that your own ability and experience are appropriate to the project and that you will enjoy the type of work involved.

Among the better known franchises in Britain are such names as Wimpy, Kentucky Fried Chicken, Dyno-Rod (drain cleaning), Pizza Express, Budget Rent-a-Car and Prontaprint (printing shops). More information can be obtained from the British Franchise Association, 15 The Poynings, Iver, Bucks SL0 9DS (tel 0753-653546). The latest figures suggest that the minimum price for a reputable franchise would be around £6000, though most will cost more and the current average price is given as £16,000. The investor who has £20,000 or more at his disposal should have quite a wide range of options to choose from. The range of franchise activities is fairly broad, covering car rental, cleaning services and retailing of domestic and leisure products as well as different kinds and scales of food service operations.

Your bank manager can obtain a bank reference and sometimes an informal opinion as well. Your solicitor will explain the implications of the contract. Your accountant will have a search made at Companies House on the parent company and will check projections and help with your personal cash flow and tax problems. They should all be

165

consulted but the commercial decision will be yours because professional advisers must err on the side of caution. If you are a good negotiator you may secure better terms than those first offered.

Government

There are many more vacancies for older people, ie over 35, than is generally realised both for 'permanent' and for 'temporary' posts with the Civil Service. Your study of newspaper advertisements in both the official appointments columns and the classified display columns will soon tell you which skills are in demand and current rates of pay. For many posts regular 'competitions' are held (administrative grade posts, factory inspectorate, statisticians and economists, etc) but applications may be considered at other times. In recent years the setting up of the prison industries has given openings for a large number of people with production expertise at almost any age (below 52). Some appointments are now on short-term contract — five years for example. As every post has to be advertised (either internally or externally or both) vacancies are not difficult to discover. General enquiries concerning the Civil Service should be addressed to: The Civil Service Commission, Civil Service Department, Basingstoke, Hants.

Local government, both at county and town hall levels, is an area well worth considering for new career possibilities. Professionally qualified people — engineers, architects, solicitors and so forth — are always in demand and salaries nowadays compare by no means unfavourably with the private sector. This is a field particularly worth looking at for people who have taken the academic part of a professional course — maybe through private study — but have not had the opportunity to complete the articles which enable them to practise professionally. Opportunities are, however, by no means confined to specialists. These days there is an increased appreciation of the kind of experience that a person with a good business background can bring to some of the town hall's more management-oriented activities, such as the administration of catering, entertainment and housing.

Another growth area in local government in recent years has been social and community work — the probation service, youth employment and organising the care of the old, the sick and the disadvantaged. It is a career that nowadays attracts a fair number of idealistic young graduates, but many local authorities would welcome a leavening of more mature people with a good all-round record and some experience of the world at large. Specialised training is, however, necessary. Fuller details of such schemes of the grants available can be obtained from The Social Work Advisory Centre, 26 Bloomsbury Way, London WC1A 2SR.

For information on local government appointments in general, write to the Clerk of the Council of the appropriate authority. In spite of Government cutbacks in capital spending, public sector jobs have continued to grow even in the current recession, especially in administrative areas of services such as the NHS where cuts have proved difficult to effect.

Lecturing and teaching

Although in the humanities and in some 'soft' social science subjects there is an over-supply of people in relation to jobs, the prospects for those qualified in technical, scientific and practical subjects are still looking good at all levels. In schools there is a very real shortage of teachers in these areas and special grants are available to mature students who wish to qualify to teach what are termed 'shortage subjects'. You will be able to get details from your local education authority. At universities and higher education establishments, too, there is a fairly high turnover of staff in technology, scientific and managerial faculties — often because they receive attractive offers from abroad or as the result of consultancy activities. While at this level it is not essential to have qualified teacher status to get a job (nor is it the case in private schools) your prospects are greatly enhanced if you do have it. A number of colleges offer special courses to mature students which lead to the award of the Teacher's Certificate of Postgraduate Education, a certificate which, by the way, also qualifies you to teach in ordinary schools. The colleges in question are:

Garnett College, Downshire House, Roehampton Lane, London SW15 4HR;
Bolton College of Education (Technical), Chadwick Street, Bolton BL2 1JW;

The Polytechnic, Holly Bank Road, Lindley, Huddersfield
HD3 3BP;
The Polytechnic, Wolverhampton, Castle View, Dudley,
West Midlands, DY1 3HR.

The requirements for admission are a combination of practical experience with a degree or a recognised professional
certificate or diploma. The Registrar of one of these colleges,
however, points out that people over 50 are unlikely to be
suitable because their academic qualifications tend to be out
of date — even if their practical experience is sound.

The courses last for a year from September and are grant-
aided for travel, tuition, residence and payments to dependants. Full details are given in the prospectuses of the colleges
listed above. Write to the Registrar.

Working abroad

Apart from the growing scope for self-employment, undoubtedly the most dynamic area of opportunity for mid-
career executives has in recent years developed abroad rather
than at home; in particular in the oil-producing countries and
some of their neighbours who have also benefited indirectly
from oil revenues. Without exception these countries have
embarked on huge modernisation programmes, involving
industrial expansion, social welfare projects of all kinds (eg
hospitals and education), and the overall provision of what is
termed 'infrastructure' — roads, airports, harbours, telecom-
munications and all the other services a modern state requires.
Quite a number of these countries have rather small popu-
lations (tiny compared to their financial resources), and
nothing like enough skilled local people to realise their
plans. Furthermore, time is not on their side. In a number of
OPEC states, oil revenues will run out by the end of the
century, so they cannot afford to wait until enough skilled
nationals are available to start to develop and build up industries and services to take over from oil.

The opportunities for skilled expatriates are therefore
considerable, as the many recruitment advertisements testify.
In the main these are in the technological, educational and
medical spheres, though there are increasing signs that a
market for more general managerial jobs is also developing —

one sees, for instance, quite a number of sales jobs being advertised these days. Opportunities for women, though, are still very limited.

Salaries are generally higher than in the UK, though the strength of sterling has narrowed the gap quite appreciably over the past couple of years. Most reasonably senior jobs begin around the £14,000 mark and at upper levels sums in excess of £30,000 are by no means uncommon. They are also, in many Middle East countries, tax free. Even in countries where this is not the case, taxes tend to be lower and a more indulgent attitude taken on claims for tax relief. Furthermore, salaries are generally augmented by what sound like very generous fringe benefits. Almost all jobs in the Middle East, Asia and Africa (at any rate north of the Zambezi) offer such things as free accommodation, usually at least six weeks' annual holiday with fares home paid, free medical attention, school fees paid or subsidised, often an end-of-contract bonus and so forth. It all sounds almost too good to be true, so where's the catch?

Basically in fact there is no catch at all, though if you are thinking of looking for a job abroad — and the best way to do this is simply to keep an eye on the recruitment pages of the national and specialist press — we have included a checklist of points to look out for in the job description or at the interview. (It is reproduced from *Working Abroad: The Daily Telegraph Guide to Working and Living Overseas*, published by Kogan Page/The Daily Telegraph.)

The main factor to bear in mind is that these generous terms of employment do reflect, in the first instance, the fact that the cost of living in these countries is very high, though the general opinion is that you can nevertheless save a lot of money by working there. Some would add that this is because there is not a great deal to spend it on and this brings us to the second point, which is that living conditions in many OPEC countries and also in posts in the developing world can be very tough: climatically unpleasant and socially restrictive or isolated — or all three. One might indeed go as far as to say that the higher the salary and the more generous the fringe benefits for equivalent jobs, the tougher the location is apt to be.

This is something you have to remember if you have a family. Surprisingly, in view of the inducements offered, the

169

turnover of staff in many overseas posts is high, mainly because of family problems. Six months a year with the temperature in the 90s and over is a very different proposition from a fortnight in the sun on the Costa del Sol. The whole business of fitting in with a totally alien culture, where familiar home comforts are either totally unobtainable or astronomically expensive, is a situation many people find it impossible to cope with. So before taking the big leap of going abroad, you should be very sure of what is involved beyond those temptingly big salary cheques.

This applies to working as well as living conditions. In the case of multinational companies, the management style does not change much from place to place, but appointees to smaller, locally based firms may find things a little less predictable, and have to cope with autocratic management, inadequate or underqualified subordinates, long working hours and even, on occasion, problems about getting paid on time. Salaries are frequently paid in local currency and are therefore subject to exchange rate fluctuations over the period of a contract — which contract is observed to the letter, with penalties for non-compliance. So it is essential to read and make sure you understand everything in it. Also, though accommodation is generally provided nowadays even if you work for a local firm, it may be below standard, or not be ready on time. In general, in fact, it is a good idea for married men to go out ahead and sort out all these problems before the family gets there.

That having been said, local firms do often pay better than British-based ones or multinationals (no odious comparisons with salaries at home) and generally offer more scope to the mid-career executive on the move. The hazards mentioned above can be greatly minimised if you do your homework properly by finding out as much as possible about the firm and the country before committing yourself.

The rest of the world, outside the emerging resource-rich areas, offers a rather bleaker picture as far as executive jobs are concerned (or others, for that matter), though changes in economic fortunes can produce sudden demands for people — and equally sudden drops in demand. Over the past two years, for instance, the rise in the price of gold has produced a boom in South Africa after a long period of recession. Singapore and Hong Kong are also experiencing fairly rapid growth as more and more manufacturing activities are moving towards the huge labour pools of the East, away from the high-cost, strife-ridden industries of the developed world. By the same token, the job market in Europe and the USA holds out few prospects except for those with expertise in computers and the information-based industries that are now rapidly coming to the fore. Technological skills, however, seem to be in demand almost everywhere and the Ministry of Overseas Development has an active recruitment programme covering British Commonwealth countries. The following is an account of how this operates.

Ministry of Overseas Development

Many British expatriates serve in the public sector in developing countries, their employment being either by the UK Government under its technical cooperation schemes or by the overseas government or other authority under British supplementation schemes (Overseas Service Aid Scheme, OSAS, or British Expatriates Supplementation Scheme, BESS).

Technical Cooperation Officers (TCOs), whose appointments are mostly advisory in nature, are appointed and paid directly by the Ministry of Overseas Development (ODM) at salary rates related to UK levels plus an inducement element; they also receive a tax-free overseas allowance calculated to cover the additional cost of living overseas and an outfit allowance. Passages (normally by air) are provided on taking up and relinquishing an appointment, and reasonable baggage and related insurance expenses are met. An interest-free advance of salary may be taken to assist, for example, with the purchase of a British car. In most cases the baggage entitlement includes car freight and insurance. Eligible children may, up to the age of 18, have two free and one contributory holiday visit passages in each period of 12 months (a small parental contribution is payable only for the third visit by the first eligible child), with one passage only for older eligible children. It is the responsibility of the local government to supply furnished accommodation. Salaries are subject to UK taxation.

Those serving under supplementation schemes (normally cadre appointments) are employed and paid by the overseas government or authority, but the British Government provides a supplement, based on UK salary levels and movements, which includes cost of living and 'inducement' elements. Passages are provided, and allowances include education, holiday visit passages (as for TCOs), medical treatment, and a loan to help with the purchase of a British car before departure. Salaries are subject to local, not UK, income tax; salary supplements are normally free of tax. It is the local government's responsibility to provide hard-furnished accommodation, and any rental payable is taken into account when calculating salary supplements.

By far the largest number of British expatriates employed under both schemes are working in Africa, and the biggest areas of recruitment are teaching (particularly secondary school teachers in English, maths and science to GCE O level), natural resources, infrastructure, and administration. The length of the assignments vary. For OSAS or BESS appointments it is usually for two to three years and may be renewable.

The Crown Agents recruit on behalf of overseas governments and various public bodies as well as for their own teams in nearly all professional and technical fields at senior levels.

An employment conditions checklist for working abroad

Salaries for jobs abroad nearly always sound like the proverbial offer you cannot refuse. Bear in mind, though, that you will incur a whole range of expenses which would not arise if you were employed here. It is vital to consider these expenses and to check whether your remuneration package covers them, either directly or in the form of fringe benefits.

If you are going to work for a reputable international company, they will probably know what the score should be. But if your employer is new to, or inexperienced in, the game of sending people to work abroad (especially if he is a native of the country to which you are going and therefore possibly not aware of expatriates' standards in such matters as housing) here are some of the factors you should look at in assessing how good the offer really is.

To help you arrive at realistic, up-to-date answers it is worth trying to get hold of someone who has recently worked in the country to which you are thinking of going, or to get a copy of *Working Abroad: The Daily Telegraph Guide to Working and Living Overseas.*

1. Is your employer going to meet the cost of travel out from the UK for your family as well as yourself?

2. Is he going to provide accommodation?
   (a) Of what standard?
   (b) How soon will it be available after you arrive?
   (c) Furnished or unfurnished? If furnished, what will be provided in the way of furniture?

3. If accommodation is not free, but there is a subsidy, how is this assessed?
   (a) As an absolute sum? In this case, is it realistic in the light of current prices? If not, is there any provision to adjust it?
   (b) As a proportion of what you will actually have to pay?

4. Who is going to pay for utilities (gas, water, electricity, telephone)?

5. If there is no subsidy and accommodation is not free, are you sure your salary, however grand it sounds, is adequate? Do not accept the job unless you are sure about this.

6. Will the employer subsidise or pay for you and your family's hotel bills for a reasonable period until you find somewhere to live? Is the figure realistic in the light of local hotel prices?

7. Will you be paid a disturbance allowance?
   (a) Is it adequate to cover the cost of shipping (and, possibly, duty at the other end) for as many household and personal effects as you are going to need?

   (b) Will your eventual return to the UK as well as your departure be taken care of?

8. What arrangements will be made:
   (a) To cover legal and other fees if you have to sell your UK home?
   (b) To cover the difference, if you have to let your UK home while you are away, between the rental in-

come and such outgoings as insurance, mortgage interest and agent's management fees? Will you be compensated for any legal expenses you incur, eg to get rid of an unsatisfactory tenant?

(c) To cover the cost of storing household effects?

9. Will you be paid a clothing allowance, bearing in mind that you will need a whole new wardrobe if you are going to a hot country? Will it cover just your clothes, or those of your family as well?

10. Will your employer pay for or subsidise household items (eg air conditioning) that you will need in a hot climate and that are not included in an accommodation package?

11. Will the employer provide/subsidise the cost of domestic servants? If not, is your salary adequate to pay for them yourself, if they are necessary and customary in the country and at the level at which you are being employed?

12. Is a car going to be provided with the job, with or without driver?

13. Will the employer pay for/subsidise club membership and/or entrance fees?

14. Will you be paid an allowance for entertaining?

15. Will the employer pay for/subsidise local school fees or UK boarding-school fees?

16. If your children attend UK boarding-schools, what arrangements are there for them to join you in the holidays? Will the employer pay for their air fares and if so, will this be for every holiday or only some of them? If the latter, can you arrange for them to be looked after at Christmas or Easter?

17. What arrangements are there for your own leaves? Do the employers provide return air fares to the UK or another country of your choice? Will they pay for your family? And for how many holidays?

18. Will the employer pay for/subsidise all or any additional insurance premiums you may incur? In some

countries (eg Saudi Arabia) it is advisable to insure your servants; or costs of motor vehicle insurance may be inordinately high because of poor roads and low driving standards.

19. If social security payments are higher than in the UK (eg in some EEC countries) will your employer make up the difference?

20. Will he contribute to your medical expenses if free medical attention is not available or inadequate?

21. If your salary is expressed in sterling would you be protected against loss of local buying power in case of devaluation?

22. Is your salary in any way index-linked to the cost of living? How often are the effects of inflation taken into account in assessing and adjusting your current level of remuneration?

23. If there are any restrictions on remittances, is your employer prepared to pay a proportion of your salary into a UK bank or that of some other country with a freely negotiable currency? This would not attract UK tax if you are away for more than 12 months.

24. Does your employer contribute towards language teaching for you and/or your wife?

Appendix A:
Writing 'on-spec' letters

Almost every managing director has one or two 'on-spec' letters addressed to him each week. Usually he glances at them and then asks his secretary to pass them on to a subordinate; at this point they usually go into one of those files that are seldom, if ever, referred to. But a letter that shows you are alert to what the company you are writing to is doing is much more likely to arouse the recipient's attention; if only for the simple and human reason that we all tend to be interested in people who show an interest in us.

For instance, you may have read a business news item about an engineering company buying a controlling interest in a German firm as part of its Common Market policy. Before long this company will be needing people in various capacities who speak German and who have a knowledge of the special problems and opportunities of operating in a Common Market country. If you have qualifications of this sort to offer your letter is likely to produce an interview even if the company concerned has not yet got around to considering what new staff it needs to handle the problems its acquisition is going to pose.

Let us take the hypothetical case of a personnel man, aged 47 or so, with a degree in German. He has always taken an interest in the labour situation in his industry as it applies in Germany, has kept abreast of the main books and articles on the subject that have appeared over there and has written the occasional piece on the subject – perhaps in a professional journal – and has talked about it to his local Chamber of Commerce or at conferences. In other words, he is not expert but he knows enough to get by and has something specific to point to. A sample letter to a company chairman or managing director might look something like this:

Dear Sir X,

I noticed in your company report in the *Financial Times* on the 17th March that your firm has recently bought a controlling interest in Süddeutsche Metallwerke GmbH. I imagine that you will be retaining the existing German management, but it occurs to me that before long you may be bringing in new policies which will require close, knowledgeable and sympathetic liaison with your German staff. As an experienced personnel manager with a degree in German and a special knowledge of German labour laws and negotiation machinery (on which I have written a number of articles) I feel I might be of particular use to you; I for my part am looking for a job that will enable me to apply my interest in comparative British and German approaches to personnel problems in a practical way.

May I come and talk to you about the possibilities? I look forward to hearing from you.

Apart from the fact that a letter like this makes it clear that the applicant (a) is taking an intelligent interest in the company he is writing to and (b) has something concretely useful to offer them, it embodies a number of other lessons which are pertinent to the on-spec approach:

1. It is fairly short, but it covers the salient points and offers enough specific information about the applicant to arouse the reader's interest.
2. It does not give away the applicant's age — there is plenty of time to do that when it is asked for.
3. It does not specifically say whether or not the applicant is currently in a job. If you are not working, do not volunteer this information. (On the other hand, if you are this is a plus point and should always be brought in. But do not do so too obtrusively, otherwise the cynical reader may assume that you have been asked to 'look around'!)
4. It concludes with a firm but polite request for action on the part of the recipient.

The point of such a letter is that while it does not include a résumé it arouses enough interest for one to be requested. This has two important advantages over the 'out of the blue' approach. First of all, having asked for a résumé, the recipient will read it, which he might not have done had it come unsolicited. Secondly, if the reader has asked you to do something — namely, prepare a full résumé — he will usually feel under some obligation to you, the least manifestation of which would be to ask you to come for an interview, whereas otherwise your age might not get you over this all-important first hurdle. Once you are in, you are in with a chance.

The example we have given is, of course, a very 'soft-sell' approach. A marketing man approaching other marketing men might want to use something with more punch. Like this, for instance:

Dear Mr Smith,

I notice in *The Caterer and Hotelkeeper* of the 3rd June that AB Foods are planning to launch a new kind of vending machine for providing self-service in hotel bedrooms. I am keen to make a move into a sphere with some real growth potential, which I feel sure this has, but apart from that I have a good deal of very relevant experience to offer you in this new venture. I started off my business career in catering and was Assistant Manager of the Grand Hotel in Aberdeen before being lured away into selling. Most recently I was Regional Manager in the Midlands for Peter Lorraine's wines division. I was in charge of a team of 18 representatives and during my time there sales rose from £250,000 to close on a million. On the ideas side, I might say it was at my suggestion that the company launched its very successful scheme of selling wine from the cask in off-licences.

May I come and see you to discuss how I can help you? I shall phone your secretary next week to find out when you are free to make a date.

The last sentence puts a foot —albeit a tactful one — in the door and would probably not be suitable if you were writing for an administrative post. But here the writer is looking for a job that involves selling and his positive attitude suggests that he is not a man who readily takes no for an answer. Notice, though, that underneath the slightly brash tone the letter is still quite specific about what the applicant has to offer in the way of experience and achievement. On the other hand, it does not go into too much detail, because the object is to whet the reader's appetite rather than to tell him the whole story. This has the further advantage that it enables you to be selective — to talk about the highlights without mentioning any troughs that might have occurred. Those will have to come out later, at the interview or when you are asked to submit a résumé (though you should avoid volunteering information about why you left this or that job). But as any mail-order man can tell you, once interest in a product has been aroused at all the first important step towards making a sale has already been taken.

Writing an effective on-spec letter is a task that should

179

not be underrated, even by those who are accustomed to expressing themselves in writing. It is a good idea, when you have prepared such a letter, to put it away for a few days and then look at it again with fresh eyes. Even better, though, is to show your letter to a friend whose judgement you trust. Don't ask him for a general opinion — which is likely to produce a general sort of answer that may err on the side of politeness — but for replies to specific questions about its effectiveness. Here are some points to check.

1. *Have you clearly identified the reason why you are writing?*

   Beware of making your approach so oblique and 'soft-sell' that the reader is left in doubt about what you are getting at. At some point you should specifically put over the fact that you are looking for a job with the firm to whom you are writing.

2. *Is your letter likely to arouse the recipient's interest and attention almost as soon as he starts reading it?*

   The best way to do this, as we have said earlier, is to appeal to his self-interest by identifying a need which you think he has or might have and showing how you can fill it. For instance, every firm has middle-management problems, needs accountants, looks for people with a proven record of sales success. As an executive you will be familiar with general personnel problems in your area of experience even if you cannot find the need that particularly applies to the firm you are writing to.

3. *Does it omit unnecessary data that will make it too long to read?*

   Bear in mind that the recipient is a busy man. He has a lot of letters on his desk that he has to read and answer.

4. *Does your letter clearly imply that you are a forward-looking man with an open mind and plenty to contribute for the future?*

   Cut out phrases that sound as though you are an old dog who can't be taught any new tricks ('a lifetime of experience in the . . . business'). Emphasise what you achieved in the job, not how long you did it for.

5. *Is the writing crisp, precise and easy to follow?*
Avoid pompous words (beware particularly those of Latin origin), long involved sentences, repetitions and near-repetitions of meaning or content.

6. *Does each sentence and each paragraph follow logically from the one before it?*
First of all, the letter must have an overall structure. It must have a beginning (why you are writing), a middle (a thumbnail sketch of your qualifications and experience), and an end (request for an interview). That is one way to lay out the contents, and probably the best one. But whichever method you choose, don't go hopping back and forth with details that are not related to each other or which are not obviously connected. In the examples we have just given, for instance, it would be rather puzzling at first reading if the writer had put: 'I started off my business career in catering and was assistant manager of the Grand Hotel in Aberdeen. Latterly I was regional manager etc.' Notice how he has linked the two jobs together with the phrase 'before being lured into selling'.

7. *Are the spelling, punctuation and grammar correct?*
You may think this is unnecessary advice, but a lot of people slip into errors, just as one tends to slip into bad driving habits: it gets you there but it doesn't follow the book. To some people who read letters of application, deviations from strictly correct English are irritating. If you're not sure of a word, look it up.

8. *If you're writing to someone by name, have you got the spelling right?*

Appendix B:
Guidelines for preparing your cv

A cv is a factual summary of you and your career to date. It can be used for any appointment when supplemented by information specific to that job. Try to keep your summary to one page (or at most two pages), if possible, following the order set out below:

Full Name

Address

Telephone Number: Home/Office

Date of Birth

Nationality

Marital Status

Education (dates, type of school/college, location and principal examinations, subjects and results)

Languages

Professional Qualifications

Career Summary (what jobs you have held and what you consider to be your most significant achievement; begin with your current or most recent job and work back)

Publications

Other Appointments/Achievements (eg JP, Member of National Export Council 19– to 19–)

Remuneration in present/most recent job (give basic salary plus bonus, special fringe benefits)

Period of Notice (ie when you would be available – omit this if not currently employed).

It is the practice of many firms and consultants to verify academic/professional qualifications and membership of professional bodies at the shortlist stage. To avoid unnecessary delay, ensure that the information you give includes the exact name of the university/professional institution, with dates and degree/membership levels.

Appendix C:
Specimen letter of application in reply to an advertised vacancy

257 Spring Gardens
Cookley
Surrey

1st February 1981

Dear Sir,

I wish to apply for the post (advertised in the *Daily Telegraph* of the 30th January) of Marketing Director of English International Airlines Limited and enclose my curriculum vitae.

I have had extensive experience in civil aviation, mostly operational, with an ever-increasing amount of administration, and have taken full advantage of courses in order to further my knowledge.

My current post is in the contract department of Southern Airlines at Gatwick, where all types of services are provided for international flag carriers, charter airlines, corporate aircraft and private aviation. With the recent increase in private small plane movements at the airport, we have been quick to realise the potential and hold a virtual monopoly in the handling of this business.

The unit has diversified over the past two years to embrace private and business operators and I have been closely concerned with negotiating and initiating methods and procedures to provide the individual service this type of customer requires.

I am commercially minded and believe in selling our service vigorously. Last year I represented the company at the Business and Light Aircraft Show at Cranfield, where we secured a lot of new business. The current climate in civil aviation has made me economically minded and I have made several suggestions to my Managing Director for cost cutting, many of which have been implemented.

I have had dealings with all levels of people in aviation, civil and military, plus the Department of Trade and Industry, Customs, Immigration and other statutory bodies.

I welcome the opportunity to become a member of a small company and know that my experience and knowledge will be beneficial to

English International Airlines and that my ideas for expansion in the future are valuable. I am very ambitious and dedicated to aviation and know that I am the man your Chairman, Group Captain Tom Higgins, is seeking to guide his company into a profitable and successful future. I believe that the potential of this type of company is enormous and look forward to being a part of that future.

Yours faithfully,

Q S Silver

Notes on how this letter has been constructed

Para 1. States the name of the post being applied for. Remember a company may be advertising more than one executive post at any one time.

Para 2. Gives a thumbnail picture, in one sentence, of the nature of the applicant's experience.

Para 3. Describes what the applicant is doing in his current appointment and shows how this relates to the job being advertised.

Para 4. Covers his experience in the immediate past, again making it clear how this relates to a marketing appointment.

Para 5. The applicant says something about the kind of person he is and backs it up with specific evidence of achievement.

Para 6. Describes the range and nature of his contacts.

Para 7. A vigorous and positive conclusion is reinforced by the fact that the applicant has managed to dig up the name of the company's chairman. It is therefore likely that he has taken the trouble to find out something about the company as a whole.

Appendix D:
Useful sources of information

Basic information on all companies has to be lodged with the Registrar of Companies (Companies House, Crown Way, Cardiff CF4 3UZ) and is available for inspection by members of the public. It will show the latest account, the balance sheet and the names, qualifications and place of birth of the directors. Charges against assets, such as mortgages, also have to be shown.

Public reference libraries in large cities, as well as the libraries of leading professional associations and institutes (such as the BIM and the IPM), carry a variety of reference works that can help you in your search and give you useful background information for interviews. Some of the principal works that may be worth consulting are listed below.

Moodies Investment Handbook will give you extracts of annual reports and chairmen's statements, profit record, share price movement, and a host of other information on companies' activities.

The Kompass Register covers some 28,000 British firms, identifying them by products and services and describing in tabular form what sort of trading activities they undertake.

Dun & Bradstreet's Guide to Key British Enterprises lists several thousand British companies, showing the address, type of activity, when founded, names of directors and the sales turnover.

Dun & Bradstreet's British Middle Market Directory is a companion volume providing similar information for 'the progressive middle sector of British industry and commerce'.

Dun & Bradstreet's International Market Guide gives names, addresses, products and services of companies in many of the leading industrial countries of the world. Frequently financial appraisals of these companies are provided.

Standard and Poor's Corporation Research gives details of the activities of the 6000 largest US firms.

The Times 1,000 List of Companies: company reports are kept on file at most reference libraries.

Extel Statistical Services are a source of financial information on both quoted and unquoted British companies. There is also the *Extel European Service*, which extends mainly to quoted European companies.

London Gazette gives information about bankruptcies and the people involved in them. Back numbers are obviously useful for checking the credentials of people or firms you feel doubtful about.

Who Owns Whom lists and cross indexes parent companies, their subsidiaries and associates.

Who's Who gives potted autobiographies of 'top people'.

The Directory of British Associations lists trade associations and chambers of commerce.

Special business surveys and supplements, both of countries and specific industries, are undertaken from time to time by leading national newspapers. The publisher's library (or public reference libraries with specialist business collections) will be able to tell you whether they have any recent surveys on any particular field. The *Economist Intelligence Unit* is particularly good in this area.

Directories, yearbooks and annuals can be a valuable source of information. *The Stock Exchange Yearbook*, for instance, gives a thumbnail financial picture of all quoted public companies. Another well-known publication, the advertisers' *Blue Book*, lists market research, direct mail and PR firms, as well as showing agencies and their clients. Many specialist professions (eg design and art directors) also publish yearbooks which can contain editorial articles with useful careers-related contents.

British Qualifications is a comprehensive survey of all qualifications in Britain, how they are obtained and through whom. It also tells you what all those letters after people's names mean — useful in interviews. Published by Kogan Page.

Prestel, the television-transmitted information service, though not as yet in widespread use, lends itself ideally to advertising for vacancies. Worth keeping an eye on developments there.

A Guide to Successful Job-Hunting: concise, sensible (and free) pamphlet issued by PER. Also contains suggestions for further reading which include *Changing Your Job* and two other Kogan Page/Daily Telegraph Guides: *Working for Yourself* and *Working Abroad*.

Appendix E:
Consultants, recruitment agencies, training centres and vocational guidance services

Consultants, recruitment agencies and vocational guidance services

The organisations listed in this first section of the appendix are coded according to the services they offer.

CC	=	career counsellors
ES	=	executive search consultants
MS	=	management/technical selection consultants
REG	=	register of executives
TEMP	=	temporary executive appointments
VG	=	vocational guidance consultants

Alexander, Hughes & Associates (UK) Ltd
De Walden Court, 85 New Cavendish Street, London W1M 7RA
01-636 9184
Chairman: A E Young
Offices in Brussels and Amsterdam and associates in France, Germany, USA, Mexico, Japan and Hawaii.
ES

John Anderson & Associates
Norfolk House, Smallbrook Queensway, Birmingham B5 4LJ
021-632 5758
ES, MS

The Arens Group
375 City Road, London EC1V 1NA
01-278 9476
Managing Director: Joseph F Arens
International — offices in Portugal.
ES

Assessment and Guidance Centre
6a Bedford Square, London WC1
01-580 3108
Psychologist: James Barrett
CC

187

ATA Selection & Management Services
Head office: 29 Basbow Lane, Bishop's Stortford, Herts
0279-506464
209 Great Portland Street, London W1N 5HG
01-637 0781
102 New Street, Birmingham B2 4HQ
021-643 1994
Equity & Law Building, 36-38 Baldwin Street, Bristol BS1 1NR
0272-211035
34 The Boulevard, Crawley, Sussex
0293-514071
Anglia House, 24-26 Frederick Street, Edinburgh EH2 2JR
031-226 5381
86 Cross Street, Manchester M2 4LA
061-832 5856
23 Cumberland Place, Southampton SO1 2BB
0703-37555
Managing Director: G Fox
MS

Charles Barker — Coulthard Ltd
30 Farringdon Street, London EC4
01-236 3011
MS

Berndtson International Ltd
28 Welbeck Street, London W1M 7PG
01-935 3470
ES

Michael Blakiston & Associates Ltd
87 Jermyn Street, London SW1Y 6JD
01-839 4786
ES

Boyden International Ltd
11 Arlington Street, London SW1
01-629 5986
Executive search consultants, operating on a worldwide basis.
ES

Bull Holmes (Management) Ltd
45 Albemarle Street, London W1X 3FE
01-493 0742
ES, MS

Business Development Consultants (International) Ltd
Ibex House, 42-47 Minories, London EC3N 1DY
01-488 0155
ES

188

Canny Bowen Associates Ltd
83 Pall Mall, London SW1Y 5ES
01-839 2561
Top executive search and appraisal.
ES

Career Analysts
Career House, 90 Gloucester Place, London W1H 4BL
01-935 5452
This is the largest and best known vocational guidance centre in the
country. The client is given aptitude, interest, personality and attitude
tests and the results are then discussed with one of their psychologists
at a consultation. A written report is sent to the client in which the
results of the tests are given and recommendations made on career
decisions. Practical help is given and a plan of action worked out.
Further help is then available as well as a follow-up two years later.
There is also a redundancy counselling service.
Fees: Up to age 34 years £80 + VAT; over 35 years £90 + VAT.
VG

Career Counselling Services
46 Ferry Road, London SW13 9PW
01-741 0335
Director: Robert Nathan
Services include consultation, counselling and testing.
Fees: £55.70 + VAT
CC

Career Plan Ltd
Chichester Chambers, Chichester Rents, London WC2
01-242 5775
Services include three tests — ability, interests and personality — and an
interview.
Fees: £70 + VAT
VG

**CEPEC (Centre for Professional and Executive Career Development and
Counselling)**
Sundridge Park, Bromley, Kent BR1 3JW
01-464 4121
Director of Counselling: Tony Milne
CC

Chusid Frederick & Co Ltd
35-37 Fitzroy Street, London W1P 5AF
01-580 7861
This company specialises in helping the executive who wishes to change
his job, and who is prepared to spend time in finding the very best. The
amount of time spent with each client varies enormously, but the
average is 4½ months. Their service involves interviews with

psychologists and counsellors. Fees vary according to the amount of
time needed to meet the client's needs.
CC

Clive & Stokes
14 Bolton Street, London W1Y 8JL
01-493 1811
ES

Wendell Clough & Associates
87 Regent Street, London W1 7HF
01-734 0931/01-839 3295
ES

Coopers & Lybrand Associates Ltd
Shelley House, Noble Street, London EC2
01-606 4040
MS

John Courtis & Partners Ltd
78 Wigmore Street, London W1
01-486 6849
ES

Criterion Appointments Ltd
13-14 Upper St Martin's Lane, London WC2H 9DL
01-836 9376
Criterion Appointments Ltd are engineering recruitment specialists to
the construction, offshore, petrochem process and electronic industry.
MS

EAL
18 Grosvenor Street, London W1X 9FD
01-499 0513
ES, MS

Philip Egerton & Associates
178 Piccadilly, London W1
01-499 2215
ES, MS

Eurosurvey Ltd
43-44 Albemarle Street, London W1X 3FE
01-409 1361
ES

Russell Ewbank & Partners Ltd
Prudential House, North Street, Brighton, Sussex BN1 1RW
0273-24892
Management and professional recruitment.
ES

Executemps
351 Oxford Street, London W1
01-629 2665
Temporary appointments for accountants.
TEMP

Executive Care Career Consultants
Palmcroy House, 387 London Road, Croydon, Surrey CR0 3PB
01-684 6101
Specialise in helping middle and senior management aged over 35 to
obtain appointments either in this country or abroad.
REG

Executive Search International Ltd
8a Symons Street, Sloane Square, London SW3 2TJ
01-730 0137/9
Managing Director: J M Reid
Assessment, international recruitment.
ES

Goddard Kay Rogers & Associates Ltd
21 Cork Street, London W1X 1HB
01-434 1744
ES

Grigor & Norcross Ltd
PO Box 5, Berkhamsted, Herts
044 27-3904
ES, MS

Robert Half Personnel Agencies (UK) Ltd
Lee House, London Wall, London EC2Y 5AS
01-606 6771
Managing Director: R W Parker
Specialists in top executive recruitment in the accountancy, financial
and banking fields.
MS

Handy Associates International Inc
148 Buckingham Palace Road, London SW1W 9TR
01-730 8176
ES

John Hearn & Partners
9 Orme Court, London W2
01-727 2755
ES

Heidrick & Struggles International
25-28 Old Burlington Street, London W1
01-734 9091
Managing Director: D W Diehl
Specialists in executive search and recruitment.
ES

Higson-Ping Ltd
110 Jermyn Street, London SW1
01-930 4196
ES

Hoggett Bowers & Partners Ltd
Sutherland House, 5 Argyll Street, London W1
01-734 6852
ES, MS

Mervyn Hughes Alexandre Tic (International) Ltd
2-3 Cursitor Street, London EC4A 1NE
01-404 5801
Chief Executive: L A Robertson
Management and executive selection.
ES

Huntercombe Associates
92 Hagley Road, Edgbaston, Birmingham B16 8LU
021-454 0958
Director: J V C Wylie
ES

Inbucon/AIC Management Consultants Ltd
Knightsbridge House, 197 Knightsbridge, London SW7 1RN
01-584 6171
Managing Director: L H Brooks
MS

Independent Assessment and Research Centre
57 Marylebone High Street, London W1M 3AE
01-486 6106
Director: Dr K M Miller
CC

InterExec Registrar Ltd
22-23 Old Burlington Street, London W1
01-434 3661
Managing Director: C Scott-Brown
CC

International Appointments (London) Ltd
Greener House, 66-68 Haymarket, London SW1Y 4RF
01-839 1602
ES

IPG Technical Recruitment Ltd
Julco House, 26-28 Great Portland Street, London W1N 5AD
01-637 0212
Specialists in selection and search.
MS

JWT Recruitment Ltd
40 Berkeley Square, London W1X 6AD
01-629 9496
Managing Director: Anthea Mallett
MS

Kiernan & Co (UK) Ltd
23 St James's Square, London SW1A 1HE
01-839 7384
ES

Korn/Ferry International
2-4 King Street, St James's, London SW1Y 6QL
01-930 5524
Managing Director: David Munns
International executive search consultants, specialising in the
recruitment of well-qualified men and women from a wide variety
of disciplines.
ES

Landsdowne Recruitment Ltd
Design House, The Mall, London W5 5LS
01-579 2282
Recruit all categories of personnel in the UK and overseas.
MS

Robert Lee International Manpower Consultants Ltd
24 Berkeley Square, London W1X 6AR
01-499 0342
ES, MS

London Executive Placement Bureau
17 Berners Street, London W1
01-580 9213
Managing Director: John Gifmar
Specialists in marketing, advertising and sales executives.
MS

Management Personnel
Registered and head office:
York House, Chertsey Street, Guildford, Surrey GU1 4ET
0483-64857
Regional office for Surrey, Sussex, Kent and Hants:
Shaw House, 2 Tunsgate, Guildford, Surrey GU1 3QT
0483-65566
Regional office for Bucks, Berks and Middlesex:
2 Eton Court, Eton, Windsor, Berks SL4 6BY
07535-54256
Regional office for Herts and Beds:
Equitable House, Ridgmonts Road, St Albans, Herts
0727-35116
Management Personnel provides a specialist service in the field of
executive recruitment and selection, covering all aspects of commerce
and industry both in the UK and overseas.
MS

Robin Marlar & Associates Ltd
14 Grosvenor Place, London SW1
01-235 9614
ES, REG

Charles Martin Associates Ltd
23 College Hill, London EC4R 2RT
01-248 1709
Senior executive selection consultants for appointments in industry,
commerce and the professions in the UK and overseas.
ES

Mills & Nuttall Ltd
Kings Langley, Herts WD4 9HE
40-66955
Director: J S Nuttall
CC

Minster Executive Ltd
28 Bolton Street, London W1Y 8HB
01-493 1309/1085
Chairman: J G Barnes
CC

MSL Group International Ltd
17 Stratton Street, London W1X 6DB
01-493 3551
International management consultants in personnel, specialising in
management and executive selection. UK regional offices in
Birmingham, Manchester, Glasgow, Edinburgh and Belfast. Overseas
companies throughout the world.
ES, MS

MSMS International
115 Mount Street, London W1Y 5HD
01-493 6807
ES

Odgers & Co Ltd
1 Old Bond Street, London W1X 3TD
01-499 8811
Recruitment specialists for top financial, general management and
marketing positions (largely based on an executive register).
ES, MS, REG

Ores International Ltd
35 Maddox Street, London W1R 9LD
01-629 4953
ES

Overton Shirley & Barry Partnership
26 Holborn Viaduct, London EC1A 2BP
01-353 1884
Senior Partner: Colin Barry
ES

Owen-Browne Associates Ltd
29 St James's Street, London SW1
01-839 4401
ES

PA International Management Consultants Ltd
Hyde Park House, 60a Knightsbridge, London SW1X 7LE
01-235 6060
MS

P-E Consulting Group
1 Albemarle Street, London W1X 3HF
01-409 2669
MS

Peat Marwick Mitchell & Co
5th floor, 1 Puddle Dock, Blackfriars, London EC4V 3PD
01-236 8000
International general management and executive selection consultants.
MS

Personnel Appointments
6-7 New Bridge Street, London EC4
01-583 5567
Principal: Mack Dinshaw
Divisions specialising in accountancy and professional appointments;
executive search division; UK and overseas.
MS

Personnel Placement Services Ltd
14a Cross Street, Reading, Berks RG1 1SN
0734-595343
Managing Director: P Flip
Selection and recruitment.
MS

Plumbley Endicott & Associates Ltd
Premier House, 150 Southampton Row, London WC1B 5AL
01-278 3117
ES

Price Waterhouse Associates
Southwark Towers, 32 London Bridge Street, London SE1 9SY
01-407 8989
MS

Reed Executive
192 Bishopsgate, London EC2M 4NR
01-283 9863
Director: George Cross
ES

Russell Reynolds Associates Inc
1 Mount Street, London W1Y 5AA
01-491 7877
ES

Sabre International Search Ltd
15 Jermyn Street, London SW1
01-998 5135
Managing Director: P A Chalkley
International, executive search and management consultants.
ES

Sanders & Sidney Ltd
5-6 Yarmouth Place, Brick Street, London W1Y 7DW
01-492 0491
Marketing Director: Theodore O Simpson
CC

Search & Assessment Services Ltd
23 High Street, Banbury, Oxon OX16 8EG
0295-59885
Chief Executive: Michael Wood
ES

David Sheppard & Partners Ltd
21 Cleveland Place, St James's, London SW1Y 6RL
01-930 8786
ES

D Simpson
5 Wykham Gardens, Banbury, Oxon
0295-51633
ES

John Stork & Partners Ltd
10 Haymarket, London SW1
01-839 4953
ES

Spencer Stuart & Associates Ltd
113 Park Lane, London W1
01-491 3866
ES

Talent Brokers Ltd
20 Maddox Street, London W1R 9PG
01-499 4288
Chief Executive: Lawrence D Auckland
Executive recruitment consultants.
ES, MS

THinc Consulting Group International (UK) Ltd
85 Jermyn Street, London SW1
01-930 2952
Regional Director: S Gurney-Randall
CC

Christopher Tilly & Associates Ltd
19 Bentinck Street, London W1
01-935 2593
ES

Touche Ross & Co
4 London Wall Buildings, London EC2
01-588 6644
MS

Tyzack & Partners Ltd
10 Hallam Street, London W1N 6DJ
01-580 2924
ES, MS

John Veale Search Associates Ltd
120 Crawford Street, London W1H 1AF
01-487 3456
ES

Vocational Guidance Association
7 Harley House, Upper Harley Street, London NW1 4RP
01-935 2600
Director: J J Lawrie
VG

Ward Howell Consulting Partners
17 Old Bond Street, London W1
01-499 6416
ES

Western Personnel Ltd
5 Berkeley Square, Clifton, Bristol BS8 1HJ
0272-291888
Recruitment and selection; executive search.
MS

West One Selection Ltd
61 Berners Street, London W1
01-636 8791
Recruitment selection specialists: managerial and executive
appointments, UK and overseas.
ES, MS

Harold Whitehead &.Partners Ltd
The Whitehead Consulting Group,
21 Wigmore Street, London W1H 9LA
01-580 0191
ES

Whitehead Mann Ltd
44 Welbeck Street, London W1M 7HF
01-486 6255
ES

Wrightson Wood Ltd
4-5 Grosvenor Place, London SW1
01-245 9871
Managing Director: Christopher Wysock-Wright
ES

Wrightson Wood (Bristol) Ltd
St Brandon's House, 29 Great George Street, Bristol BS1 5QT
0272-214499
ES

Egon Zehnder International
87 Jermyn Street, London SW1Y 6JD
01-930 9311
ES

Management education and training centres

Anglian Regional Management Centre
Constituent institutions:
North East London Polytechnic, Essex County Council
Contact: B A Littlewood
024-541 2141
Courses are offered at Danbury Park, Chelmsford, and at Duncan
House, High Street, Stratford, London E15 2JB
01-590 7722

East Midlands Regional Management Centre
Derby Lonsdale College of Higher Education, Kedleston Road,
Derby DE3 1GB
Contact: A R Syson, Head of Division of Management Studies
0332-31681
Leicester Polytechnic, PO Box 143, Leicester LE1 9BH
Contact: F A Mee, Head of School of Management
0533-50181
Trent Polytechnic, Burton Street, Notts NG1 4BU
Contact: A Rogers, Head of Department of Management Studies
0602-48248

Kingston Regional Management Centre
Kingston Polytechnic, Gypsy Hill Centre, Kingston Hill,
Kingston-on-Thames KT2 7LE
Contact: T A Swinden, Director
01-546 2181

London Regional Management Centre
Constituent institutions:
Polytechnic of Central London
City of London Polytechnic
Polytechnic of North London
Polytechnic of the South Bank
South West London College
Thames Polytechnic
Cordwainers Technical College
South Thames College
Southwark College
Hackney College
Hammersmith and West London College
Paddington College
South East London College
Contact: Patrick J O'Brien, Head, London Regional Management
Centre, 311 Regent Street, London W1R 8AL
01-637 7583

Northern Regional Management Centre
Sunderland Polytechnic
Teesside Polytechnic
Newcastle Polytechnic
Contact: J W Gritton, Director, Durwin House, Washington Town
Centre, Tyne and Wear NE38 7ST
0632-471150

North West Regional Management Centre
Woodland Centre, Southport Road, Chorley, Lancs TR7 1QR
025 72-66942
Director: E K Langham
Constituent institutions:
Greater Manchester School of Management
Merseyside and Cheshire School of Management
Lancastrian School of Management

Southern Counties Regional Management Centre
Contact: The Dean, Portsmouth Polytechnic,
141 High Street, Portsmouth PO1 2HY
0705-812611
Director: Stanley Hyman

South West Regional Management Centre
Bristol Polytechnic, Coldharbour Lane, Bristol BS16 1QY
0272-656261
Contact: P W Holmes, Head

Thames Valley Regional Management Centre
Slough College of Higher Education, Wellington Street, Slough,
Berks SL1 1YG
0753-33680
Contact: M B Brodie, Dean
Constituent institutions:
Oxford Polytechnic
Buckinghamshire College of Higher Education
Slough College of Higher Education

Welsh Regional Management Centre
The Polytechnic of Wales, Pontypridd, Mid Glamorgan CF37 1DL
0443-405133
Contact: Dr F J Hybart, Director

West Midlands Regional Management Centre
North Staffordshire Polytechnic, College Road, Stoke-on-Trent
0782-45531
Contact: A J H Kitley, Head

Yorkshire & Humberside Regional Management Centre
Residential Management Studies Centre,
17-21 Westbourne Road, Broomhill, Sheffield S10 2QQ
0742-66284/667051
Contact: M B Cumbers, Director

Late Entries

A H Cornwall
545 Chancery House, Chancery Lane, London WC2A 1QU
01-831 6925
Executive career and re-employment counselling.
CC

Executive Preselectors Ltd
8a Symons Street, Sloane Square, London SW3 2TJ
01-730 0137
Director: J M Reid
Professional, technical and management recruitment.
MS

Forty-Plus Career Development Centre
High Holborn House, 49-51 Bedford Row, London WC1V 6RL
01-242 4875/6
Managing Director: Pauline Hyde
A career counselling centre providing comprehensive professional
assistance to redundant executives in the middle and upper
management levels.
CC

Overseas Recruitment Services
37 Golden Square, London W1R 4AL
01-439 9481
Managing Director: Tony Reeves
ES, MS, TEMP

Index of Advertisers